500 Essential Vocabulary Words for the ISEE & SSAT

For Upper & Middle Level Students

A tutoring guide by
Upwards Tutoring Co.

SSAT is a registered trademark of the Secondary Admission Test Board, and ISEE is a registered trademark of the Educational Records Bureau. Neither sponsor nor endorse this book.

To access your free flashcards, please visit our website:

UpwardsTutor.com

We offer essay support, personal tutoring, and free resources for a number of entrance assessments, including:

SAT
ACT
ISEE
SSAT
SHSAT

Table of Contents

Congratulations!

If you're reading this page, you've already taken the first step towards improving your ISEE or SHSAT verbal scores. Regardless of which test you take, having an advanced and broad vocabulary is an important component of getting your best score. In this book, we walk you through the expert tips and secret tricks of scoring high on the verbal section of the test.

Why do the verbal sections of these tests need their own study guide? Simply put, you either know the vocabulary necessary to ace the test or you do not. **The amount of advanced vocabulary you could be tested on is over one thousand words,** and even though some books might teach you the tricks and tips, very few books offer you a full list of the vocabulary you could be tested on. This book is meant to bridge that gap. If you use it consistently and loyally, you're likely to know the first 500 essential vocabulary words necessary for acing the test.

We encourage you to check out our website for complementary flashcard sets that you can use during and after you've practiced in this workbook. If you use these resources, we believe that you will accomplish great growth.

We believe in you.

About Upwards Tutoring Co.

Upwards Tutoring Co. has been in existence since 2016, when we started tutoring students in grades 4-12 for high-stakes tests. Our tutors come from ivy and elite colleges, such as the University of Pennsylvania, the University of Michigan, and the University of California-Los Angeles. They are former teachers and expert test-takers who know what it takes to support students through transformative growth.

When Upwards was founded, we noticed a serious flaw in the work of many other elite tutoring services: a drop-and-go approach that dumped test-taking tips on students without teaching them how to integrate those tips into their test-taking practices effectively. These tutoring companies offered impersonal services that stand in the face of what research says matters for student learning: relationships and iteration. Upwards was founded as a remedy to this. We use cycles of teaching and monitoring to continuously improve your child's score. We measure improvement frequently to craft data-driven strategies personalized to each student, and we do it all while prioritizing the importance of relationships between tutors, students, and parents.

Since 2017, we've expanded our services. We now offer support on the ISEE, SHSAT, SSAT, SAT, ACT, and the college admissions process. Our students have gained entrance into competitive, top-tier institutions. For more information, please see our website: **upwardstutor.com.**

How to Use This Wordbook

This workbook is structured in five sections. We know the temptation to dig in and skip to the practice. But remember, this is not a sprint. This is a marathon. We encourage you to take a slower approach to give yourself time to absorb the vocabulary. After all, many of the vocab words that students are tested on in the ISEE or SSAT are also words they will see on college admissions tests, like the SAT or ACT. If you take your time now in learning these words, you'll be in a better place when you begin to prepare for those tests later on.

This book is organized in the following sections:
1. **Overview:** This is what you're reading right now. This section is meant to teach students how to use this workbook, teach families how they can support their students, and answer any questions you may have.
2. **Bootcamp:** In the Bootcamp section, we lay out the essential tips and tricks that we return to throughout the book. Do not skip this section! It's got all the strategies necessary for achieving your best score. In this session, we walk you through how to use prefixes, suffixes, and context clues to get every single question correct.
3. **Vocab and Practice**: The vocabulary of the book is structured in 20 sections. Each section has 25 words and a set of practice questions.
4. **Wrap up:** We conclude with some final practice and some next steps to get you ready before the big test.
5. **Glossary:** This section contains all 500 words in one easy-to-find list.
6. **Write-you-own:** You may come across new words in your school, your reading, or other practice tests. Write them down in this section.

Why is the book structured this way?
The answer is simple: Science, or rather, the science of learning. Research says that vocabulary takes time and continued practice. It takes a combination of reading, writing, and talking to be able to learn and retain vocabulary knowledge. Research also says that the more vocabulary students try to learn in a small amount of time, the less likely that knowledge will be both sticky and deep. We want sticky knowledge that you can retain for a long time. We want deep knowledge so you can recognize a word no matter the question it shows up in. Doing small bursts of new words and practice, and then returning to the new words with flashcards, helps us make sure that we're reading, writing, and speaking new words so as to make your learning sticky and deep!

If you still have questions, take a look at the Q & A section on the next page.

Q&A: Your Questions Answered

- **How much should I be studying vocab a week?**
  That depends—how much time do you have? When we work with students preparing to take the ISEE or SSAT, we typically recommend starting a year beforehand. Vocab takes time to learn, and students differ in how quickly they're able to absorb new words. What we recommend is that students start studying vocab 6-12 months ahead of the test. There are 1000 vocab words to learn. This workbook will get you started with the first and most essential 500 words. If you have 52 weeks before the test, your student will need to learn roughly twenty words a week. Some students can accomplish this in three 20 minute practice sessions, either with this book or with the flashcards you can find on www.upwardstutor.com.

- **I have a limited time before the test. What should I do?**

  There are two important things to do:

  1. **Review the Workshop sections of this book**: You can't learn 500 words in two weeks. But you can learn the best practices for making an educated guess when you don't recognize the vocabulary. You can find an overview of these best practices in the Workshop sections.

  2. **Do whatever practice you can**: Because of the way that the SSAT and ISEE are scored, even getting one additional question right can really improve your score on the verbal section. So, if you have 24 hours until you take the test, try to learn thirty words. If you have a week, try to learn 130 words. A small amount of vocabulary practice may have a huge impact on your verbal scores.

- **I'm a parent. How can I support my student?**
  Flip the page. We offer a number of suggestions for parents in our next section.

- **Do you offer any other supports for the ISEE and SHSAT?**
  Yes! We offer a range of tutoring services for many different tests and a growing list of resources on www.upwardstutor.com.

A Note to Parents

We know that high-stakes testing can be a stressful time for parents and families. You've already taken the first step in helping your student prepare for the test in seeking out resources that can support their growth. We've noticed when parents help to structure and encourage student's practice, student scores benefit.

For parents who're looking for tips to support their students in the test preparation process, we've compiled some best practices that we believe correlate to student success on the ISEE and SSAT.

- **Encourage Daily Practice**: Thirty minutes a week is not enough to transform your student's score, but 10-30 minutes a weekday can help to ensure that your child is prepared. Vocab is a particularly practice-heavy component of the test. You either know the vocab words, or you don't. In order to know the words, you need to see them, practice them, and eventually memorize them by heart. There are over 1000 words students should know in order to maximize their chance of getting the highest score possible. Even if a student memorized 25 words a week, it would still take 20 weeks. This is a tall order, but a habit of daily practice can help to make the task more manageable.

- **Use Flashcards:** We've created flashcard sets for all 500 words in this book, which you can access as a free resource on our website. We encourage students to first learn and do the practice problems in this book. However, the research on learning vocabulary has shown the importance of speaking and continued practice. By doing some frequent and consistent flashcard practice with your student, you can increase the chance that they can recognize and deeply understand the meaning of the word rather than forget it a few weeks after they've seen it in this book.

- **Review the Workshop Sections:** Often, students want to rush past the Workshop sections to get straight to the practice of this book. Encourage them to slow down and point out the important strategies that live in the Workshop sections. Knowing these strategies can benefit students on any admissions test, whether it's the ISEE, SSAT, SAT, GRE, etc.

- **Encourage Vocab Use:** The hallmark of true vocabulary knowledge is the ability to use the word outside of flashcards and this book. If your student uses the word "fast," prompt them to use a newly-learned word from this book, like "agile." If your student uses the word "stubborn," encourage them to use the word "obstinate," which is also found in this book. By practicing flashcards with them, you'll be better able to prompt them to use the words they are learning in everyday life.

We encourage you to visit our **www.upwardstutor.com**, where we have many checklists, guides, and practice tests to help you and your student prepare for the big test.

About the ISEE Test

The Independent School Entrance Exam, or ISEE, is an admissions test for many private and independent schools. While there are different ISEE tests for different grade levels, this book is designed for Middle and Upper Level test-takers. Students who are currently in grades 6 or 7 will take the Middle Level test, while students currently in grades 8-11 will take the Upper Level test. The format, but not the content, of both tests are identical.

Section	Time
Verbal Reasoning	40 questions (20 minutes)
Quantitative Reasoning	37 questions (35 minutes
Break	5-10 minutes
Reading Comprehension	36 questions (35 minutes)
Mathematics Achievement	47 questions (40 minutes)
Break	5-10 minutes
Essay	1 essay (30 minutes)
Total Time	2 hours 50 minutes – 3 hours

The Verbal Reasoning Section:
The verbal reasoning section is composed of two question types: synonyms and sentence completions. By teaching you the vocabulary you're likely to see on the ISEE, this book can help you ace the synonym questions. Each synonym question has four answer choices (A, B, C, D).

It's important to move quickly through the verbal section. With 40 questions in twenty minutes, you have approximately thirty seconds per question! Knowing the vocabulary in this book will help to ensure that you're not losing time because you've never seen a word before.

Scoring:
Students are graded on this test by grade level. This means that even though a sixth grader will take the same test as seventh graders, their score will only be compared to students in the sixth grade.

When a student completes ISEE, the number of right and wrong answers are computed to give a raw score that is then converted into a scaled score. For the verbal section, the scale scores are in the range of 760-940 for both Middle Level and Upper Level test takers. The scaled score isn't really meaningful in itself. This is because your scaled score is then converted into a percentile rank, which compares your score to all the scores of all other students in your grade level who took the test in the last three years. If you're in the 90th percentile, you scored better than 90% of all other test-takers in your grade level from the last three years.

Often, you hear people talk about getting a number between 1-9 on the ISEE. This is because your percentile rank is converted into a stanine score. Typically, a score of a 7-9 is considered a good score because it is considerably above average.

Percentile	Stanine
1-3	1
4-10	2
11-22	3
23-39	4
40-59	5
60-76	6
77-88	7
89-95	8
96-99	9

This book is intended to support your growth on the verbal reasoning section. For more resources on other sections, please visit www.upwardstutor.com.

About the SSAT Test

Like the ISEE, the Secondary School Admission Test (SSAT), is a required part of the application process for many private and independent schools. While there are different SSAT tests for different grades, this book is designed for Middle and Upper Level test-takers. Students who are currently in grades 5-7 will take the Middle Level test, while students currently in grades 8-11 will take the Upper Level test. The format, but not the content, of both tests are identical.

Section	Time
Writing Sample	1 essay (25 minutes)
Break	5 minutes
Quantitative	25 questions (30 minutes)
Reading	40 questions (40 minutes(
Break	10 minutes
Verbal	60 questions (30 minutes)
Quantitative	25 questions (30 minutes)
Experimental	16 questions (15 minutes)
Total Time	3 hours, 5 minutes

The Verbal Section:
The verbal section is composed of two question types: synonyms and analogies. By teaching you the vocabulary you're likely to see on the SSAT, this book can help you ace the synonym questions. Each question has five answer choices (A, B, C, D, E). This makes it a bit more difficult than the ISEE because you need to eliminate four wrong answers, rather than three wrong answers.

It's important to be moving quickly through the verbal section. With 60 questions in thirty minutes, you have approximately thirty seconds per question! Knowing the vocabulary in this book will help to ensure that you're not losing time because you've never seen a word before.

Scoring:
Students are graded on this test by grade level. This means that even though a fifth-grader will take the same test as sixth and seventh graders, they'll be graded according to their level and aren't expected to get as many questions right as students in the higher grades.

When a student completes the SSAT, the number of right and wrong answers is computed to give a scaled score. For the verbal section, the scale scores are in the range of 440-710 for Middle Level test takers and 500-800 for Upper Level test takers. The scaled score isn't really meaningful in itself. The scaled score for the SSAT is converted into two sets of percentile ranks:
1) How your score compares to all other students
2) How your score compares to those in your grade level and those who have identified as the same gender as you

This can be confusing for students. But the important thing to know is that the higher your percentile in either set, the better your chance of getting into your dream school. Don't let the scoring complexity throw you off your game. The important thing is to keep practicing so you can watch your score on SSAT practice tests increase over time.

You do get penalties on the SSAT for getting questions wrong. This means that students have to balance their confidence in an answer with the feeling of not wanting to get the answer incorrect. One way to maximize your chance of success and minimize your chance of penalties on the verbal section is to learn and practice the vocabulary in this book. The more vocabulary you know, the more confident you'll be in your answer choices.

This book is intended to support your growth on the verbal section. For more resources on other sections, please visit www.upwardstutor.com.

Bootcamp: Synonym Questions

On both the SSAT and ISEE, students must answer synonym questions. A synonym is a word that is similar to another word. For example, *happy* is a synonym for *glad*. You know plenty of synonyms. For example:

- *Quick* and *fast*
- *Angry* and *mad*
- *Think* and *reflect*

The synonyms you see on the SSAT and ISEE are much more difficult. It's not uncommon that you'll get a question that looks like this:

1. Ponder
    a. Petulant
    b. Ruminate
    c. Lacerate
    d. Laudatory

Even if you only recognized one of the words, it still would make it very difficult to get the right answer. This is why it is so important to learn and practice vocabulary before the test. If, at this point, you don't recognize any of the words, don't worry! Most students don't know these words at first. In order to learn them, they do exactly what you're doing now: they practice!

Answering Synonym Questions Correctly:

At Upwards we teach a three-step process for answering synonym questions. We've found that students who follow this process are much more likely to get questions correct. The three steps are:

1. Define the given word
2. Use your strategies: cognates, known phrases, prefixes, and similar words to make an educated guess about the meaning of the word
3. Use process of elimination

Before we dig into this three-step process, we need to make sure you understand the strategies in Step 2.

Strategies

If you don't know a word and are having trouble finding its synonym, there are several strategies you can use to help you make an educated guess. We call these strategies:

1. Cognates
2. Known Phrases
3. Prefixes
4. Similar words

We'll review each to make sure that you know how to use the strategy on the test.

Cognates

When students have experience with languages other than English, it can be a huge help! Lots of words from other languages are similar to English words. We call these cognates. For example, one Spanish word is *Ceremonia*. Can you guess what this means? If you guessed *ceremony*... you're right! They look and sound very similar.

Knowing another language can come in handy on the test because you could use your language skills to make an educated guess. For example, a common SSAT & ISEE word is *sympathetic*. This sounds very similar to a Spanish word: *sympatico*. In Spanish, *sympatico* means nice. If you didn't know the word *sympathetic*, but did know the word *sympatico*, you could guess that *sympathetic* has a similar definition to "nice." And you'd be correct! *Sympathetic* means "likable" or "friendly."

Known Phrases

Sometimes you may have heard a word but don't really know its meaning. For example, you may have heard the term "essential worker," but you don't know the dictionary definition of the word *essential*. You can use your knowledge of the phrase to help you make an educated guess about the meaning of a word.

If you know that essential workers are very important workers in our society, such as doctors, grocery store clerks, and those who deliver the mail, you can probably correctly guess the answer to the following questions.

1. Essential
    a. Apt
    b. Necessary
    c. Suitable
    d. Existential

Because essential workers play a necessary role in our society, we can guess that *Essential = Necessary*.

Prefixes

Prefixes are so important to making educated guesses. A prefix is the beginning part of a word, and often it contains a clue about the word's meaning. In the word *benevolent*, the prefix is *bene-*. If a word starts with the prefix *bene-,* it usually means that the meaning of the word is related to something good or positive.

For example:
Benevolent = good-hearted and kind
Benefit = a good result
Beneficial = resulting in something good

If you see a word that starts with *Bene-,* you can be very confident that the synonym should be a positive word.

Now you try:
   1. Benefactor
        a. Curmudgeon
        b. Panacea
        c. Simplistic
        d. Helper

If you guessed *Helper*, you're correct! Helpers are people who try to have a positive impact on a project or circumstance. Even if you didn't know the other definitions, you could guess using the prefix *Bene-* that *Benefactor* and *Helper* are synonyms.

Similar Words
In this final strategy, you always try to look for similar words that can help you make an educated guess about the right answer.

For example, what if you came across this question on the test:

   1. Grandeur
        a. Silent
        b. Extravagance
        c. Garrulous
        d. Imperious

Even if you didn't know what the definition of *grandeur* meant, you could use two of your strategies to get this question correct:

   1. **Look for a similar word for *grandeur*.** Grandeur sounds like "grand." Grand means something that is large or important. We're looking for a word that has something to do with being very big or very important.

   2. **Use prefixes in the answer choices.** The prefix for *Extravagance* is *Extra-.* When something is extra, it is more than what we need. This means that is a lot of something. Grand and extra are similar words; they both involve a large or larger number of something.

Therefore, the correct answer is *Grandeur. Grandeur* means grand elegance, or a lot of elegance. *Extravagance* means wealthy and luxurious. Look at how they're used in these sentences:
   • The grandeur of the palace was breathtaking.
   • The extravagance of the palace is breathtaking.

Both words have definitions that involve a lot of *something*. In the case of the two sentences above, both words signal that the palace has a lot of breathtaking beauty.

Let's you try:

Now that you know the strategies, let's look at an example of a synonym question.

1. Palatial
    a. Impregnable
    b. Horrible
    c. Robust
    d. Magnificent

If we follow the steps, we can make an educated guess about the right answer.

Step 1: Define the Given Word	At first glance, you may not recognize the word palatial. If you can't define it, move on to Step 2.
Step 2: Use Your Strategies	What does *palatial* sound like? It sounds like the word *palace*. Palaces are most often very large or beautiful castles where wealthy royalty live. Keep this image of a palace in your head. We'll use it to help us in our process of elimination.

Step 3: Use Process of Elimination	Now we see if we can eliminate answer choices and pick the correct answer.
	
	1. Palatial:
	    a. Impregnable
	    ~~b. Horrible~~
	    c. Robust
	    d. Magnificent
	
	Right away, we can eliminate option B. The image of a palace and the word *horrible* just don't fit.
	
	Even if you don't know the definition of the words *impregnable* or *robust*, you can still make an educated guess that *Palatial* is a synonym for *Magnificent*. *Magnificent* means impressive or beautiful, just like the typical image of a palace. Therefore, we can guess that palatial means something similar. Like magnificent, palatial means impressively beautiful.

Bootcamp: Sentence Completion

The ISEE verbal section has two types of questions:
1) Synonyms
2) Sentence Completion

For more information on synonyms, see the previous section. If you're not taking the ISEE, feel free to skip ahead. The SHSAT doesn't have any sentence completion questions.

Answering Sentence Completion Questions Correctly
Roughly half of the questions in the Verbal Reasoning section are Sentence Completion questions. These questions are arranged by difficulty so that the first sentence completion question is the easiest while the last sentence completion question is intended to be the most difficult. Sentence Completion questions are often easier for students because they have context to help you choose the right answer. If you follow a tried-and-true method for Sentence Completion questions, you're likely to see your score increase. We call this the RPP method.

Read	Read the sentence. While reading, underline or circle any clues. No question is impossible, and all questions are specifically designed to have clues that can tell you if the missing word is positive or negative, a noun or an adjective, etc.
Predict	Use the clues to predict a word that might fit in the blank.
Process of elimination	Use process of elimination. After reading all answer choices, cross out the two most likely to be incorrect answer choices. Then ask yourself: out of the two best remaining answer choices, which is *best*.

Let's try one together

The ballerina's _____ dancing _____ the audience.
a. Lithe, awed
b. Graceful, bored
c. Audacious, dulled
d. Simplistic, entranced

Read	What clues did you underline? The **ballerina's** _____ dancing _____ the **audience.** • Ballerina = Ballerinas are known for their graceful moves. The missing word is probably a positive adjective • Audience = The word that comes before *audience* must be something about *the effect the* dancing has on the audience. The word is probably a positive verb.
Predict	Use the clues to predict a word that might fit in the blank. The ballerina's **graceful** dancing **impressed** the audience.

Process of elimination	After reading all answer choices, ask yourself: "What two answer choices are most clearly wrong?"
	
	The ballerina's _____ dancing _____ the audience.
	   e. Lithe, awed
	   f. ~~Graceful, bored~~
	   g. ~~Audacious, dulled~~
	   h. Simplistic, entranced
	
	F is most likely not correct. If a ballerina is graceful, we would expect them to engage the audience rather than bore the audience. G is most likely not correct. Even if we don't know that *audacious* means bold or outrageous, it is unlikely that the dancing dulls or bores the audience.
	
	What about E and H? Both *awed* and *entranced* mean that the audience is engaged! The deciding factor is between lithe and simplistic. But what if you don't know what those words are? Well, simplistic sounds like simple. We can take an educated guess that if a ballerina is doing simple moves, they're probably not that interesting. H is probably not correct.
	
	The correct answer is E. Lithe means graceful, and awed means wowed. The sentence would read like this:
	
	The ballerina's **lithe** dancing **awed** the audience.

Was this difficult? Did you find yourself confused because you didn't know the vocabulary in the answer choices?

If so, that is normal. Take a deep breath. In the next section, you'll begin to dig into 500 essential vocabulary words for the SSAT and ISEE.

Learning Each Vocab Word:

In this section, you'll encounter your first set of 25 essential vocab words! Each vocab word is structured in the same way. They all look like the example below!

Begin vocabulary practice by reading the word and its definition.

Then look at how the word is used in a sentence. This will help you understand the word.

Cautious
(adj). Careful

When sneaking a snack in class, the student knew they needed to be cautious of their teacher's watching eyes and listening ears.

Word family: caution, cautioning
Synonyms: watchful, wary

_____

_____

_____

_____

Word family can help you recognize other versions of the same word you might see on the test. Reviewing these words will give you a better idea of all the forms the word can take.

The **Synonyms** provided are words that might show up in the Synonym questions on the test.

Practice writing the word in your own sentence. Research has shown that writing the vocabulary word down in a sentence you create can help you remember the word better

The First Set: Abdicate – Agitate

Directions: Read the vocab word card. Then write your own sentence using the vocab word.

Abdicate

(v.) to give up power

The king decided to abdicate the throne so his daughter could be queen.

Word family: abdication
Synonyms: resign, quit

_____

_____

_____

_____

Abhor

(v.) to hate

I abhor the taste of tomatoes.

Word family: abhorrent
Synonyms: detest, contempt, somber

_____

_____

_____

Abhorrent

(adj.) horrible, worthy of being hated

Her poor behavior at the party was abhorrent

Word family: abhor
Synonyms: loathsome, abominable

_____

_____

_____

Abominable

(adj.) horrible or unpleasant

The decision to get rid of summer vacation was abominable.

Word family: abomination
Synonyms: loathsome, detestable, hateful

_____

_____

_____

Abridge

(v.) to shorten in length or duration

Although the original book was 1000 pages, the abridged version was only 200 words.

Synonyms: shorten

_____

_____

_____

Absolve

(v.) to free from guilt or blame

The judge ruled that he was not guilty, legally absolving him from guilt.

Word family: absolving
Synonyms: liberate, forgive

_____

_____

_____

_____

Abstinence

(n.) to refrain from indulging in something

Abstinence from smoking is the best way to avoid lung cancer.

Word family: abstain
Synonyms: self-restraint

_____

_____

_____

_____

Abundant

(adj.) plentiful

The table was abundant with food. It was going to be a delicious meal.

Word family: abundance
Synonyms: bounty, abundance

_____

_____

_____

_____

Abyss

(n.) a bottomless pit

Even though he ate so much, he was still hungry. It was like his stomach was an abyss.

Synonyms: pit, chasm

_____

_____

_____

_____

Academic

(adj.) having to do with school or education

A more academic word for "show" is "illustrate."

Word family: academia, academic
Synonyms: scholastic, educational, scholarly

_____

_____

_____

_____

Acclimate

(v.) to adapt to a new climate, environment, or situation

I'm from sunny California. When I moved to Alaska, I needed to acclimate myself to the freezing cold.

Synonyms: adapt, adjust

_____
_____
_____
_____
_____

Accord

(n.) agreement

They signed an accord to ensure peace.

Word family: according
Synonyms: agreement, pact, treaty

_____
_____
_____
_____

Accrue

(n.) to grow or to gather over time

If you save a dollar a week, your savings will accrue over time.

Synonyms: grow, accumulate, amass

_____
_____
_____
_____

Adage

(n.) an old saying usually considered to be true

There is an old adage my grandmother used to say, "Eat to live, not live to eat."

Synonyms: saying, proverb

_____
_____
_____
_____

Adamant

(adj.) stubborn and persistent

She adamantly believed that she was right, and the teacher was wrong.

Synonyms: obdurate, obstinate

_____
_____
_____

Adept

(adj.) skillful

When it came to geometry, she was an adept problem-solver.

Synonyms: expert, talented, gifted

_____

Adhere

(v.) to stick to something

To win the game, they needed to adhere to the coach's game plan.

Word family: adhesion, adhesive, adherence
Synonyms: sticky

_____

Adhesion

(n.) something that is sticky or used to hold things together

Glue is an adhesion that holds things together.

Word family: adhere, adhesive, adhering, adherence
Synonyms: sticky substance, glue

_____

Adjunct

(adj.) additional

My science teacher was adjunct faculty and did not work for the school full time.

Synonyms: additional, extra

_____

Admiring

(adj.) regarding with approval or respect

She gave an admiring look at her role model.

Word family: admire, admiration
Synonyms: applauding, praising

Admonish

(v.) to warn or reprimand someone firmly

My parents admonished me for eating junk food for dinner.

Word family: admonishing, admonishment
Synonyms: scold

_____

_____

_____

_____

Adverse

(adj). unfavorable, challenging

Driving was dangerous due to the adverse conditions of rain and wind.

Word family: adversity
Synonyms: dangerous, challenging

_____

_____

_____

_____

Aggravate

(v.) to make worse

Adding fuel is sure to aggravate the fire.

Word family: aggravation, aggravating
Synonyms: annoy

_____

_____

_____

_____

Aggregate

(v.) the sum or combination of multiple parts

The aggregate of 1 + 1 is 2.

Word family: disaggregate, aggregation
Synonyms: sum, total, combination

_____

_____

_____

_____

Agitate

(v.) to disturb or upset

The agitating noise made it difficult to do homework.

Word family: agitate, agitation, agitating
Synonyms: disturb

_____

_____

_____

_____

Directions:

Fill in the blanks using the words in the box. No word should be used more than once.

If you need help, first write the definition next to the vocab word in the box. Then find the best sentence for the word.

Abdicated	Abhor	Admire	Adhere	Adept	Academic	Adjunct

Acclimate   Aggregate   Admonished

1. My teacher _____ me for not doing my homework.

2. When I moved, it took a few weeks for me to _____ to my new school.

3. In school, my favorite _____ subject is English.

4. On a field trip, it's important to _____ to the teacher's directions or else you

   might get lost.

5. The Queen _____ the throne.

6. I _____ the smell of garlic. It makes my nose hurt.

7. I am a very _____ football player. My team chose me to be the team captain.

8. The _____ of 5 and 6 is 11.

9. The substitute teacher was an _____ member of the school community.

10. I _____ my mom because she is so strong and smart.

Directions:
Select the best synonym for the vocabulary word.

1. Abhorrent
   a. Salvation
   b. Curmudgeon
   c. Detestable
   d. Lyrical

2. Abominable
   a. Misanthropic
   b. Abhorrent
   c. Putrid
   d. Abundant

3. Abridge
   a. Riot
   b. Shorten
   c. Prefect
   d. Abdicate

4. Absolve
   a. Agitate
   b. Aggravate
   c. Curtail
   d. Forgive

5. Abstinence
   a. Aggregate
   b. Restraint
   c. Miserly
   d. Agitate

6. Abundant
   a. Plentiful
   b. Stubborn
   c. Faithful
   d. Abdicate

7. Abyss
   a. Merry
   b. Pit
   c. Amass
   d. Sustain

8. Accrue
   a. Accumulate
   b. Materialize
   c. Chasm
   d. Detest

9. Accord
   a. Placebo
   b. Defeat
   c. Challenge
   d. Agreement

10. Adage
    a. Emphasis
    b. Proverb
    c. Stubborn
    d. Worsen

11. Adamant
    a. Obdurate
    b. Industrious
    c. Sticky
    d. Archaic

12. Adhesion
    a. Glue
    b. Capability
    c. Agitation
    d. Restraint

13. Adversity
    a. Abbreviation
    b. Challenge
    c. Martyrdom
    d. Excellence

14. Aggravate
    a. Simplify
    b. Improve
    c. Aggregate
    d. Worsen

15. Agitate
    a. Aggregate
    b. Adamant
    c. Annoy
    d. Bastion

Find the answer key for all sections on page 171

The Second Set: Ail—Artifice

Directions: Read the vocab word card. Then write your own sentence using the vocab word.

Ail
(v.) to suffer from sickness or pain

Her broken arm ailed her.

Word family: ailment
Synonyms: trouble, pain

_____

_____

_____

_____

Akin
(adj.) related to

Guilt is an emotion akin to shame.

Word family: kin
Synonyms: alike, similar

_____

_____

_____

Allege
(v.) to declare, usually without proof

They alleged that the mayor stole a large amount of money from the city.

Word family: allegedly, allegation
Synonyms: claim, assert

_____

_____

_____

_____

Aloof
(adj.) keeping a distance

She was aloof at parties, preferring to keep her distance from others.

Synonyms: distant, withdrawn

_____

_____

_____

_____

Altruistic
(adj.) doing good for others

Their decision to donate their birthday presents to the orphanage was altruistic.

Word family: altruism
Synonyms: generous, philanthropic

_____

_____

_____

_____

Amass
(v.) to gather together or accumulate

If you save a dollar a week, your savings will amass over time.

Synonyms: accumulate, grow

Ambiguous
(adj.) vague or unclear

The teacher's directions were ambiguous, which caused confusion.

Word family: ambiguity
Synonyms: vague, debatable

Ambivalent
(adj.) having opposite or mixed feelings (such as love and hate)

She was ambivalent towards history class. Sometimes she loved it, sometimes she hated it.

Word family: ambivalence
Synonyms: indecisive, uncertain

Ameliorate
(v.) to make better

Stephan tried to ameliorate his friend's bad mood with a funny joke.

Synonyms: improve, better

Amiable
(adj.) friendly or good-natured

Julia and Rosalia were friends. Their relationship was amiable.

Synonyms: pleasant, genial, congenial

Amorphous

(adj.) without shape

The shapeshifter was amorphous.

Synonyms: shapeless

_____

_____

_____

_____

Analytical
(adj.) intending to understand something

In their analytic essay, they analyzed the theme of the novel.

Word family: analyze, analytic
Synonyms: critical, scholarly

_____

_____

_____

_____

Anguish
(n.) suffering or pain

She began to cry in anguish.

Synonyms: despair, sorrow

_____

_____

_____

_____

Animosity
(n.) hostility

There was animosity between the rival sports teams.

Synonyms: hostility, malevolence, resentment

_____

_____

_____

_____

Antagonize
(v.) to annoy or provoke

The loud, yappy dog antagonized the neighbors.

Word family: antagonist, antagonism
Synonyms: aggravate

_____

_____

_____

_____

Antics

(n.) foolery; unpredictable behavior

His classroom antics earned him detention.

Synonyms: pranks, escapades

_____

_____

_____

_____

Apathetic
(adj.) lack of feeling or interest

Riordan's apathetic behavior towards his schoolwork caused him to neglect his homework.

Word family: apathy
Synonyms: indifferent, unconcerned

_____

_____

_____

_____

Appall
(v.) to be horrified

I was appalled by his behavior.

Word family: appalling
Synonyms: horrify, shock

_____

_____

_____

_____

Aptitude
(n.) ability

Her mathematical aptitude helped her solve difficult math problems.

Synonyms: capability, talent

_____

_____

_____

_____

Archaic
(adj.) very old

The book was so archaic that the pages were turning to dust.

Synonyms: ancient

_____

_____

_____

Arduous

(adj.) hard to do, requiring much effort

Building a house is an arduous task.

Synonyms: strenuous, taxing, difficult

Arid

(adj). very dry

The climate in the desert is arid.

Synonyms: very dry

Aristocratic

(adj.) of noble birth; snobbish

Because of his aristocratic background, he was used to fine dining and elegance.

Word family: aristocrat, aristocracy
Synonyms: noble, elite

Articulate

(v.) clearly express

She won the debate because she articulated her argument so well.

Word family: articulating
Synonyms: eloquent, communicative

Artifice

(n.) deception or trickery

Loki's artifice caused pain and problems for many.

Word family: artificial
Synonyms: trick, deceit

Directions:

Fill in the blanks using the words in the box. No word should be used more than once.

If you need help, first write the definition next to the vocab word in the box. Then find the best sentence for the word.

Amass	Altruistic	Amiable	Animosity	Antagonize	Appalled
	Archaic	Aristocrat	Arid	Arduous	

1. I was _____ by my brother's bad behavior.

2. Cooking bread can be a long and _____ process, involving a lot of mixing and prep-work.

3. I have an _____ relationship with my cousin. We get along really well.

4. The Arizona desert is particularly _____.

5. My school building is so _____ that paint chips off the wall and we don't have air conditioning.

6. You could hear _____ in the bully's voice when she demanded "give me your lunch money."

7. The goal of the game is to try to _____ as many points as possible. The more points you get, the more likely you will win.

8. I felt very _____ when I donated all my Christmas presents to the local children's hospital.

9. The _____ was used to fine dining and elegant events.

10. My little sister likes to _____ me by calling me mean names.

Directions:
Select the best synonym for the vocabulary word.

1. Ail
   a. Hue
   b. Hurt
   c. Hungry
   d. Happy

2. Akin
   a. Stationary
   b. Related
   c. Vague
   d. Indifferent

3. Allege
   a. Assert
   b. Lie
   c. Meander
   d. Elegy

4. Aloof
   a. Clarity
   b. Simple
   c. Shy
   d. Righteous

5. Ambiguous
   a. Scarce
   b. Vague
   c. Directionless
   d. Ambivalent

6. Ambivalent
   a. Testy
   b. Amiable
   c. Uncertain
   d. Unconcerned

7. Ameliorate
   a. Improve
   b. Isolate
   c. Center
   d. Specify

8. Amorphous
   a. Shapeless
   b. Zany
   c. Vague
   d. Hostile

9. Analytical
   a. Educational
   b. Critical
   c. Cursory
   d. Antagonizing

10. Anguish
   a. Sympathy
   b. Anger
   c. Pain
   d. Pleasure

11. Antic
   a. Escapade
   b. Liberation
   c. Salvation
   d. Ability

12. Apathy
   a. Horror
   b. Trickery
   c. Cruel
   d. Indifference

13. Aptitude
   a. Capability
   b. Additional
   c. Difficulty
   d. Eloquent

14. Articulate
   a. Eloquent
   b. Snobbish
   c. Taxing
   d. Ancient

15. Artifice
   a. Fake
   b. Deceit
   c. Simple
   d. Bias

Find the answer key for all sections on page 171

The Third Set: Ascent—Berate

Directions: Read the vocab word card. Then write your own sentence using the vocab word.

Ascent

(n.) movement upward; a climb

The ascent up Mt. Everest is arduous and dangerous.

Word family: ascend, ascending
Synonyms: climb, rise

_____

_____

_____

_____

Aspirant

(n.) someone who wants to achieve great things

The political aspirant decided to run for president.

Word family: aspire, aspirational, aspiration
Synonyms: dreamer, goal-getter, candidate

_____

_____

_____

_____

Assailable

(adj.) vulnerable

She didn't have armor on the battlefield, which made her assailable.

Word family: assail, assailant
Synonyms: defenseless, weak

_____

_____

_____

_____

Assert

(v.) to state a point of view

During the debate, she asserted her position.

Word family: assertive
Synonyms: declare, contend, claim

_____

_____

_____

_____

Assess

(v.) to evaluate or determine the worth of something

The teachers gave a test to assess the students' learning.

Word family: assessing, assessment
Synonyms: evaluate, test, judge

_____

_____

_____

Assiduously

(adv.) hardworking

She worked assiduously on her science project.

Word family: assiduous
Synonyms: diligently, laboriously

_____
_____
_____
_____

Astute

(adj.) smart or clever

The astute detective was known for solving difficult cases.

Synonyms: quick-witted, sharp

_____
_____
_____
_____

Attain

(v.) to achieve

It can be difficult to attain a perfect GPA.

Word family: attainment
Synonyms: achieve, accomplish

_____
_____
_____
_____

Audible

(adj.) able to be heard

A whisper is barely audible.

Synonyms: loud, clear

_____
_____
_____

Augment

(v.) to make larger

Even though she had a small allowance from her aunt, Rosa wanted to augment her income by getting another job.

Word family: augmentation, augmenting
Synonyms: increase, supplement

_____
_____
_____
_____

Authentic
(adj.) genuine and true

For my birthday, we went to an authentic Thai restaurant.

Word family: authenticate, authenticity
Synonyms: real, true, genuine

Authoritative
(adj.) having authority

To calm the excited class down, the teacher spoke with an authoritative voice.

Word family: authority
Synonyms: commanding, strong

Baleful
(adj.) harmful or menacing

A baleful storm ruined the neighborhood, tearing down trees and flooding houses.

Synonyms: menacing, wicked

Banal
(adj.) unoriginal and boring

The material presented in class was banal.

Synonyms: boring

Barbed
(adj.) spiked

The barbed wire was meant to keep intruders out.

Word family: barb
Synonyms: spiky, spiked

Barrage
(n.) an overwhelming event or thing happening

When she announced a pop quiz, the teacher received a barrage of questions.

Synonyms: bombardment, flood

_____

Bashful
(adj.) shy

They became bashful every time they were asked to speak in public.

Synonyms: timid, shy

_____

Bedevil
(v.) to cause a lot of trouble

The class clown bedeviled the class with jokes and pranks.

Word family: bedeviling
Synonyms: harass, torment

_____

Begrudge
(v.) to be reluctant or resentful

I begrudgingly cleaned my room.

Word family: begrudgingly
Synonyms: resent

_____

Belie
(v.) to give a false idea

Elephants may seem gentle, but their appearance belies that they can be dangerous.

Synonyms: contradict

Belligerent

(adj.) hostile and aggressive

The bully was belligerent towards the other students.

Synonyms: hostile, aggressive, combative, antagonistic

_____

Beneficial

(adj). resulting in something good

When you're sick, medicine and sleep are usually beneficial.

Word family: benefits, beneficiary
Synonyms: helpful, useful, advantageous

_____

Benevolence

(n.) goodness

The older woman was known around the community for her benevolence. She was always willing to help out a neighbor.

Word family: benevolent
Synonyms: goodness, kindness, compassion

_____

Benign

(adj.) harmless

At first, I thought it was poison ivy, but then I realized it was just a benign plant.

Synonyms: gentle, safe

_____

Berate

(v.) to scold sharply

My aunt berated me for not helping with dinner.

Word family: berating
Synonyms: admonish, rebuke, reprimand

Directions:

Fill in the blanks using the words in the box. No word should be used more than once.

If you need help, first write the definition next to the vocab word in the box. Then find the best sentence for the word.

Ascended Assailable Assessed Asserted Authentic Baleful
Barbed Bashful Bedeviled Berated

1. My older brother _____ me for stealing his sneakers

2. The bird _____ into the air.

3. At first, I thought the gold coin was _____ but then I realized it was a fake.

4. On our math test, my teacher _____ our knowledge of fractions.

5. One tip of the arrow has a feather, but the other tip is _____.

6. When I meet new people, I can be _____ and quiet.

7. Without a rain jacket, I was _____ to the rain.

8. The doctor _____ that the medicine was safe.

9. The bully gave me a _____ look.

10. The bees _____ me, swarming around my face.

Directions:

Select the best synonym for the vocabulary word.

1. Aspiration
   a. Inspiration
   b. Energy
   c. Pedigree
   d. Goal

2. Assiduous
   a. Diligent
   b. Intelligent
   c. Amorphous
   d. Obtainable

3. Astute
   a. Gloomy
   b. Timid
   c. Tepid
   d. Shrewd

4. Attainment
   a. Achievement
   b. Surround
   c. Malice
   d. Toil

5. Audible
   a. Loud
   b. Audio
   c. Overwhelming
   d. Kinesthetic

6. Augment
   a. Matriculate
   b. Articulate
   c. Work hard
   d. Enlarge

7. Authoritative
   a. Commanding
   b. Boring
   c. Shrewd
   d. Aggressive

8. Banal
   a. Shy
   b. Boring
   c. Confusing
   d. False

9. Barrage
   a. Half-hearted
   b. Flood
   c. Dramatic
   d. Guilt

10. Begrudge
    a. Bedevil
    b. Hesitant
    c. Gentle
    d. Resent

11. Belie
    a. Falsify
    b. Serendipitous
    c. Prophetic
    d. Overwhelm

12. Belligerent
    a. Sympathetic
    b. Aggressive
    c. Deterrent
    d. Hesitant

13. Beneficial
    a. Helpful
    b. Malignant
    c. Important
    d. Garrulous

14. Benevolence
    a. Sorrow
    b. Violent
    c. Goodness
    d. Feverish

15. Benign
    a. Spirited
    b. Wired
    c. Harmful
    d. Harmless

Find the answer key for all sections on page 171

The Fourth Set: Bewilder—Circumspect

Directions: Read the vocab word card. Then write your own sentence using the vocab word.

Bewilder

(v.) to confuse

The students were bewildered by the decision to stop serving pizza in the cafeteria.

Word family: bewilderment
Synonyms: perplex, befuddle

_____

_____

_____

_____

_____

Bias

(n.) favoring one side or opinion over another

I was biased towards my favorite team.

Synonyms: partisan, prejudiced

_____

_____

_____

_____

Blight

(n.) a disease or problem

Pollution is a blight on our society.

Synonyms: disease, affliction

_____

_____

_____

_____

Bolster

(v.) to strengthen

I listen to my favorite song to bolster my confidence before the big game.

Synonyms: support, reinforce

_____

_____

_____

Brackish

(adj.) having a salty taste and being unpleasant to drink

After taking one sip, I spit out the brackish water.

Synonyms: briny

_____

_____

_____

Brash
(adj.) bold in a rude or pushy way

Joseph's brash behavior was unlikable.

Synonyms: rude, bold

_____
_____
_____
_____

Brig
(n.) the prison of a ship

The prisoner was locked in the brig.

Synonyms: jail, prison

_____
_____
_____
_____

Briny
(adj.) salty

After taking one sip, I spit out the briny water.

Word family: brine
Synonyms: brackish

_____
_____
_____
_____

Browbeat
(v.) to intimidate

"You won't get your way, even if you try to browbeat me."

Synonyms: bully

_____
_____
_____
_____

Burgeoning
(adj.) growing

There was a burgeoning sense of excitement as the holidays approached.

Synonyms: increasing, developing

_____
_____
_____

Burly

(adj.) very stocky and muscled

The big burly man took up a lot of room in the cramped train.

Synonyms: well-built, sturdy

_____

_____

_____

_____

_____

Cacophony

(n.) jarring and unpleasant sounds

When the stack of plates fell, there was a cacophony of sound.

Word family: cacophonous
Synonyms: noise, racket

_____

_____

_____

Calamity

(n.) disaster

Covid-19 was a calamity.

Word family: calamitous
Synonyms: tragedy

_____

_____

_____

Candid

(adj.) honest

Sometimes it can be hard to give candid feedback because you're afraid the person will get angry with you.

Word family: candor, candidly
Synonyms: truthful

_____

_____

_____

Candor

(n.) honesty

When I gave my teacher feedback, they thanked me for my candor.

Word family: candid, candidly
Synonyms: truth

_____

_____

_____

Capricious

(adj.) unpredictable and impulsive

Her decision to spend all her money on a pair of shoes was capricious.

Word family: capriciousness, caprice
Synonyms: fickle, inconstant, mercurial, impulsive

Cast away

(v.) 1) to throw away 2) to be abandoned after a shipwreck

She cast away her old clothes.

Word family: cast
Synonyms: 1) throw away, 2) shipwrecked

Castigate

(v.) to scold or criticize someone severely

The group was castigated for cheating on the test.

Word family: castigated, castigating
Synonyms: reprimand, admonish, rebuke

Cautious

(adj.) careful

When sneaking a snack in class, I needed to be cautious so that my teacher didn't hear or see me.

Word family: caution, cautioning
Synonyms: watchful, wary

Chagrin

(n.) embarrassment, disappointment

Much to my chagrin, my parents came to the school dressed in clown costumes.

Synonyms: distress, embarrassment, humiliation

Chasm
(n.) 1) a deep opening in the earth's surface 2) a large difference between two things

The Grand Canyon is a famous chasm.

Synonyms: gulf, rift, schism

_____

_____

_____

_____

Choleric
(adj). bad-tempered

The bad weather made him choleric and unfriendly.

Word family: cholera
Synonyms: irritable, grumpy

_____

_____

_____

_____

Chronicle
(n.) a record of something in chronological order

The Chronicles of Narnia is a book that follows a family in a magical land.

Synonyms: account, record

_____

_____

_____

_____

Circulate
(v.) 1) to move around freely, 2) to spread widely

The newspaper was circulated widely.

Word family: circulatory
Synonyms: flow, spread

_____

_____

_____

_____

Circumspect
(adj.) unwilling to take risks

Make sure to be circumspect about giving away your personal information on the internet.

Synonyms: careful, cautious, wary, prudent

_____

_____

_____

_____

Directions:

Fill in the blanks using the words in the box. No word should be used more than once.

If you need help, first write the definition next to the vocab word in the box. Then find the best sentence for the word.

Bewildered   Biased   Blight   Bolster   Brackish   Brig
Cacophony   Cast Away   Circulated   Cautious

1. When rock-climbing you need to be extra _____. One wrong move and you could fall off the cliff.

2. On old ships, the _____ was a terrible place with hardly any light and nowhere to use the bathroom.

3. I might be _____, but I think my friends are the best.

4. Someone _____ a mean rumor about the teacher.

5. There was a _____ of noise from the marching band.

6. I decided to _____ my old jacket. It was too small for me.

7. When swimming in the ocean, I accidentally swallowed the _____ water.

8. Global warming is a _____ upon our planet, but with better environmental policies we can fix it.

9. I was _____ by the school's decision to cancel soccer practice. It seemed like an arbitrary decision.

10. I wanted to _____ my chance of winning the game by practicing hard and eating healthy.

Directions:

Select the best synonym for the vocabulary word.

1. Brash
   a. Authoritative
   b. Bold
   c. Playful
   d. Chartreuse

2. Briny
   a. Brackish
   b. Muscular
   c. Prudent
   d. Unhappy

3. Browbeat
   a. Commanding
   b. Peruse
   c. Bully
   d. Grimace

4. Burgeoning
   a. Petulant
   b. Growing
   c. Irritable
   d. Critical

5. Burly
   a. Strong
   b. Serious
   c. Weak
   d. Winnowed

6. Calamitous
   a. Serious
   b. Significant
   c. Wondrous
   d. Disastrous

7. Candid
   a. Truthful
   b. Whimsical
   c. Petty
   d. Benevolent

8. Candor
   a. Righteous
   b. Honesty
   c. Good-hearted
   d. Playful

9. Capricious
   a. Unpredictable
   b. Critical
   c. Unpleasant
   d. Intolerable

10. Castigate
    a. Hostility
    b. Snobbish
    c. Scold
    d. Achieve

11. Chagrin
    a. Disappointment
    b. Sympathy
    c. Sorrow
    d. Joy

12. Chasm
    a. Abyss
    b. Nutritional
    c. Sorrow
    d. Unclear

13. Choleric
    a. Fertile
    b. Annoyed
    c. Cautious
    d. Weepy

14. Chronicle
    a. Newspaper
    b. Novel
    c. Fiction
    d. Record

15. Circumspect
    a. Wary
    b. Pleasant
    c. Suspicious
    d. Spectacle

Find the answer key for all sections on page 171

The Fifth Set: Clandestine—Contempt

Directions: Read the vocab word card. Then write your own sentence using the vocab word.

Clandestine
(adj.) secretive

The CIA agent needed to be clandestine.

Synonyms: secret, covert

_____

_____

_____

_____

Clarity
(n.) the quality of being easy to see or understand

When the clouds cleared, I could see the skyline with clarity.

Synonyms: transparent, clear

_____

_____

_____

_____

Coalesce
(v.) to come together

When the school bell rang, the students coalesced in the hallway.

Word family: coalescing
Synonyms: unite, emerge

_____

_____

_____

_____

Coerce
(v.) to force

The parents tried to coerce their child to eat vegetables with punishment and promises.

Synonyms: compel, persuade

_____

_____

_____

_____

Cognizant
(adj.) having knowledge or being aware

She was cognizant of the dark clouds. She began to be fearful that the picnic would be stormed on.

Word family: cognize, cognizance, cognizable
Synonyms: aware, conscious

_____

_____

_____

_____

Cognize
(v.) to know

The scholar cognized the complex theory.

Word family: cognizant, cognizance, cognizable
Synonyms: understand, think, perceive

_____

_____

_____

_____

Commencement
(n.) the beginning of something

The commencement of a road trip usually starts by filling the car with gas.

Word family: commence
Synonyms: beginning

_____

_____

_____

_____

Communal
(adj.) shared

They ate a communal meal as a family.

Word family: commune
Synonyms: shared, together

_____

_____

_____

_____

Competent
(adj.) good enough

She was a competent swimmer, but not good enough to join the school swim team.

Word family: competence
Synonyms: capable, adequate

_____

_____

_____

_____

Complacency
(n.) the feeling of being satisfied with how things are and not wanting to change them

She felt a sense of complacency with her B- in math class. She didn't want to work harder for an A.

Word family: complacent
Synonyms: self-satisfaction, laziness

_____

_____

_____

_____

Composure
(n.) calmness

Though I was angry at first, I regained my sense of composure.

Synonyms: self-control

_____

Comprehensive
(adj.) including all or everything

The test was comprehensive of everything we learned throughout the year.

Synonyms: all-inclusive, exhaustive

_____

Concede
(v.) to give in or surrender

The opponent conceded the boxing match by tapping out.

Word family: concession
Synonyms: give up

_____

Condescend
(v.) to act as if you are better than someone

It's rude to condescend to someone.

Word family: condescending
Synonyms: patronize

_____

Condone
(v.) to forgive or disregard an offense

I cannot condone rudeness.

Word family: condoning
Synonyms: accept, excuse

Confinement

(n.) being restricted or kept in a certain place

Quarantine is a kind of confinement.

Word family: confine, confined
Synonyms: imprisonment, enclosed, restricted

_____

_____

_____

_____

Conform

(v.) to mold to meet some expectation

Many teenagers conform to peer pressure.

Word family: conformity, conformist
Synonyms: obey

_____

_____

_____

_____

Confound

(v.) to puzzle or confuse

Some math problems are so difficult that they confound me.

Word family: confounding
Synonyms: muddle, bewilder

_____

_____

_____

_____

Congeal

(v.) to thicken, or change from liquid to solid

As the oatmeal cooled, it began to congeal.

Synonyms: solidify, coagulate

_____

_____

_____

_____

Congenial

(adj.) agreeable

Their conversation was congenial. They agreed to be friends.

Word family: congeniality, genial
Synonyms: pleasant

_____

_____

_____

_____

Conscientious

(adj.) characterized by extreme care and great effort

My teacher expects us to complete our homework conscientiously.

Word family: conscience, conscientiousness
Synonyms: diligent, industrious

Consensus

(n). an agreement

They came to a consensus about a plan.

Word family: consent
Synonyms: accord, pact

Console

(v.) comfort

I try to console my friend when he is sad.

Word family: consolation
Synonyms: comfort, support

Construe

(v.) to interpret

I construed her actions as aggressive.

Word family: misconstrue
Synonyms: interpret, understand

Contempt

(n.) extreme dislike or disdain

His voice was full of contempt as he yelled at her.

Word family: contemptuous
Synonyms: scorn, dislike

Directions:

Fill in the blanks using the words in the box. No word should be used more than once.

If you need help, first write the definition next to the vocab word in the box. Then find the best sentence for the word.

Clandestine	Clarity	Coalesced	Cognizant	Comprehensive	Congenial
	Consensus	Console	Construe	Contempt	

1. Even though it was nighttime, the moon lit up the sky and I could see everything around me with

   _____ .

2. When I got detention, I was overwhelmed with feelings of _____ for my

   teacher.

3. I was _____ of the changing weather, noticing how the storm clouds were

   beginning to turn the sky dark.

4. My friends tried to _____ me after I got a bad grade on my test.

5. I really like to be prepared, so I made a _____ list of all the things I would

   need to pack for the overnight field trip.

6. There was general _____ among the class; we all agreed that we liked our

   new teacher.

7. She gave me a _____ smile and I knew we would become friends.

8. Every day at 5pm, the streets become crowded with cars as people _____ on

   their route home.

9. The secret agent had a _____ mission.

10. Though the book was difficult, I was able to correctly _____ its

    main idea.

Directions:

Select the best synonym for the vocabulary word.

1. Coerce
    a. Authoritative
    b. Force
    c. Fail
    d. Reticence

2. Cognize
    a. Become
    b. Think
    c. Worry
    d. Cogent

3. Commencement
    a. Initialization
    b. Graduation
    c. Finale
    d. Collaboration

4. Communal
    a. Malice
    b. Verbal
    c. Garrulous
    d. Shared

5. Competent
    a. Capable
    b. Competitive
    c. Partisan
    d. Complete

6. Complacency
    a. Laziness
    b. Calmness
    c. Detailed
    d. Introspective

7. Composure
    a. Wily
    b. Zenith
    c. Undertaken
    d. Control

8. Concede
    a. Condescend
    b. Surrender
    c. Win
    d. Deceive

9. Condescend
    a. Pallid
    b. Patronize
    c. Paltry
    d. Partisan

10. Condone
    a. Accept
    b. Obey
    c. Overwhelm
    d. Imprison

11. Confinement
    a. Confusing
    b. Imprisonment
    c. Important
    d. Acknowledgement

12. Conform
    a. Accept
    b. Listen
    c. Uniform
    d. Obey

13. Confound
    a. Bewilder
    b. Betray
    c. Contradict
    d. Constant

14. Congeal
    a. Thicken
    b. Congregate
    c. Portray
    d. Obstruct

15. Conscientious
    a. Adept
    b. Diligent
    c. Rampant
    d. Accepting

Find the answer key for all sections on page 171

The Sixth Set: Contemptuous—Demure

Directions: Read the vocab word card. Then write your own sentence using the vocab word.

Contemptuous
(adj.) expressing disdain or extreme dislike

She could sense her classmate's anger by the contemptuous look on his face.

Word family: contempt
Synonyms: disdainful, scornful

_____

_____

_____

_____

Contentious
(adj.) inclined to fight or argue

The two presidential candidates debated the contentious topic.

Word family: contention
Synonyms: debatable, controversial

_____

_____

_____

_____

Contiguous
(adj.) lying side by side

I can easily pass a note to my friend in class because our desks are contiguous.

Synonyms: adjacent, adjoining, bordering

_____

_____

_____

_____

Contradict
(v.) to force

The weatherman promised sunny weather, but he was contradicted by clouds in the sky.

Word family: contradict, contradictory
Synonyms: deny, challenge, oppose

_____

_____

_____

_____

Contrite
(adj.) feeling regret for bad behavior

She was contrite after lying.

Word family: contrition
Synonyms: remorseful, regretful, sorry

_____

_____

_____

_____

Contrition
(n.) deep regret for doing something wrong

She felt contrition after lying.

Word family: contrite
Synonyms: remorse, regret, sorrow

Conventional
(adj.) traditionally, ordinary

The conventional way to bake a cake is in the oven.

Word family: convention
Synonyms: typical, normal

Cordially
(adv.) politely

I was greeted cordially by my teacher on the first day of school.

Word family: cordial, cordiality
Synonyms: polite, pleasant, friendly

Corpulent
(adj.) overweight

He was a large, corpulent man.

Word family: corpulence
Synonyms: obese

Correlation
(n.) a connection between facts or events

There is a correlation between getting sick and cold weather.

Word family: correlative
Synonyms: connection, association

Counsel

(v.) to give advice

Her teacher counseled her to take physics instead of biology.

Word family: counselor
Synonyms: advice, guidance

_____

Crevice

(n.) a narrow crack, especially in a rock

A rat lived in a small crevice in the basement wall.

Synonyms: crack

_____

Cumulative

(adj.) increasing through successive addition

The math test was cumulative and would cover everything from the quarter.

Word family: accumulate, accumulating
Synonyms: increasing, growing

_____

Debilitating

(adj.) weakening, harmful

She had a debilitating fear of public speaking.

Word family: debilitate
Synonyms: weakening

_____

Debunk

(v.) to prove false

They used their science project to debunk the myth.

Word family: debunking
Synonyms: expose, discredit

Decompose

(v.) to rot or decay; to break down

After the leaves fall, they begin to decompose on the forest floor.

Word family: decomposition, decomposing
Synonyms: decay, break down

Decree

(n.) an order or a command

The city decreed a curfew at 6pm.

Synonyms: order, edict, command

Deduce

(v.) to draw a conclusion from facts

She could deduce he was unhappy from the frown on his face.

Synonyms: infer

Defer

(v.) to delay

He was thinking about deferring college so he could spend a year working and saving money.

Word family: deferment
Synonyms: detain

Deferment

(n.) the act of delaying

He was thinking about a deferment of college so he could spend a year working and saving money.

Word family: defer
Synonyms: detention

Deficient
(adj.) lacking

Because her body was vitamin-deficient, she was often sick.

Word family: deficit
Synonyms: lacking, insufficient

Deft
(adj). skillful

He was a deft hockey player.

Word family: deftly
Synonyms: dangerous, detrimental

Deleterious
(adj.) harmful

Poison is deleterious to your health.

Synonyms: dangerous, detrimental

Delusion
(n.) a false opinion or idea

It was a delusion to believe she could finish all her homework in thirty minutes.

Word family: delude, delusional
Synonyms: deception

Demure
(adj.) reserved

She was normally demure in her classes and preferred to sit quietly in the back.

Synonyms: shy, meek

Directions:

Fill in the blanks using the words in the box. No word should be used more than once.

If you need help, first write the definition next to the vocab word in the box. Then find the best sentence for the word.

Cordially	Cumulative	Crevice	Decomposes	Defer	Deleterious
	Contradicted	Correlation	Counsel	Delusional	

1. An earthquake shook the ground so much that it left a large _____ in the sidewalk.

2. The invitation was very polite and read, "You are _____ invited to our party."

3. As a plant _____, it becomes dirt and mud.

4. Eating too much sugar can be _____ to your health.

5. Whenever I am making a big decision, my mom tries to _____ me.

6. There is a _____ between dark storm clouds and rain. Usually, dark storm clouds are followed by rain.

7. When I was little, I believed that fairies were real. This was _____ of me.

8. Learning math is _____; you need to know fractions before you can learn algebra.

9. I decided to _____ going to college so I could work for one year.

10. Even though my parents told me I was grounded, I _____ them by going out with my friends.

Directions:
Select the best synonym for the vocabulary word.

1. Contemptuous
   a. Authoritative
   b. Disdainful
   c. Sadness
   d. Zany

2. Contentious
   a. Debatable
   b. Sympathetic
   c. Athletic
   d. Contented

3. Contiguous
   a. Pleasant
   b. Conventional
   c. Regretful
   d. Bordering

4. Contrite
   a. Regretful
   b. Parallel
   c. Controversial
   d. Benign

5. Contrition
   a. Patriotic
   b. Wispy
   c. Remorse
   d. Choleric

6. Conventional
   a. Frolic
   b. Authentic
   c. Normal
   d. Relic

7. Corpulent
   a. Overweight
   b. Wistful
   c. Empathetic
   d. Allergic

8. Deferment
   a. Advice
   b. Understand
   c. Lack
   d. Delay

9. Debilitating
   a. Mythical
   b. Weakening
   c. Difficult
   d. Boring

10. Debunk
    a. Contradict
    b. Command
    c. Expose
    d. Laud

11. Decree
    a. Order
    b. Understanding
    c. Skill
    d. Degree

12. Deduce
    a. Infer
    b. Ordain
    c. Disdain
    d. Disagree

13. Deficient
    a. Lacking
    b. Debatable
    c. Adjoining
    d. Decay

14. Deft
    a. Polite
    b. Adept
    c. Deny
    d. Scorn

15. Demure
    a. Exposed
    b. Shy
    c. Muscular
    d. Adjacent

Find the answer key for all sections on page 171

The Seventh Set: Deplorable—Elaborate:

Directions: Read the vocab word card. Then write your own sentence using the vocab word.

Deplorable
(adj.) horrible

Rocky's boss was deplorable. Rocky wanted to quit every day.

Word family: deplore
Synonyms: abhorrent

_____

_____

_____

_____

Derelict
(adj.) abandoned, ruined

There was a derelict shack on the edge of town.

Word family: dereliction
Synonyms: run down, neglected

_____

_____

_____

_____

Despair
(n.) a feeling of absolute hopelessness

When he heard the bad news, he was filled with despair.

Word family: despairing
Synonyms: hopelessness, distress

_____

_____

_____

_____

Detain
(v.) to stop or hold back

In detention, you're detained after all the other kids have left school.

Word family: detention
Synonyms: confine, delay, refrain

_____

_____

_____

_____

Detention
(n.) the act of keeping back or detaining

In detention, you're held back after all the other kids have left school.

Word family: detain
Synonyms: confinement

_____

_____

_____

_____

Deteriorate

(v.) to worsen

As her condition deteriorated, the doctors were worried.

Word family: deteriorating
Synonyms: decline

_____

_____

_____

_____

Detractor

(n.) a critic

The film had many detractors, who complained it was the worst movie they had ever seen.

Word family: detract
Synonyms: critic

_____

_____

_____

_____

Dexterity

(n.) skill or quickness

Her teacher praised her mental dexterity at the spelling bee.

Word family: dexterous
Synonyms: agility, skill

_____

_____

_____

Dignity

(n.) the quality of being worthy of esteem or respect

After the game ended, she showed dignity by shaking her opponent's hand.

Synonyms: honor, integrity, respectability

_____

_____

_____

Dilute

(v.) to weaken the strength of something, especially by adding water to a solution

My mom says apple juice is too sweet, so she makes me dilute it by adding water.

Word family: diluting
Synonyms: weaken, water down

_____

_____

_____

Dingy
(adj.) dirty, dull, or shabby

The room in the abandoned building was dingy.

Synonyms: gloomy, dark, dismal

_____

_____

_____

_____

Discern
(v.) to see clearly, to recognize

The judge couldn't discern what was true and what was false, which made it difficult to make a ruling.

Word family: discerning
Synonyms: insightful, knowledgeable, astute

_____

_____

_____

_____

Discredit
(v.) to reject as false

The politician tried to win the debate by discrediting her opponent.

Word family: credit
Synonyms: disprove, invalidate

_____

_____

_____

Disingenuous
(adj.) insincere

Even though he was smiling, I thought his smile seemed disingenuous.

Synonyms: fake

_____

_____

_____

Debunk
(v.) to criticize or speak badly of

It's rude to disparage someone behind their back.

Word family: disparaging
Synonyms: belittle

_____

_____

_____

Disposition
(n.) personality

She had a happy disposition and had many friends.

Synonyms: nature, temperament

Dispute
(n.) argument

The two neighbors were in a longstanding dispute over money.

Word family: disputation
Synonyms: debate

Distort
(v.) to bend or twist something out of its normal shape

Heat can distort the shape of a plastic container.

Synonyms: twist, bend, change

Dormant
(adj.) temporarily inactive

The dormant volcano was safe to be around.

Synonyms: resting, asleep

Dread
(n.) overwhelming fear or to be very afraid

I dreaded swim class. I was afraid of the water.

Word family: dreadful
Synonyms: fear

Dubious
(adj.) doubtful

His claim was dubious, and I had the feeling he was lying.

Word family: doubt
Synonyms: uncertain, suspicious

_____
_____
_____
_____

Dynamic
(adj). energetic, full of movement

Life in the big city is dynamic; there is always some new thing to do, eat, or see.

Synonyms: energetic, always changing, exciting

_____
_____
_____
_____

Egoist
(n.) a self-centered or conceited person

The egoist was not well liked by his peers.

Word family: ego, egotist, egotistical
Synonyms: narcissist, self-centered

_____
_____
_____
_____

Egress
(v.) to exit

A barrier blocked the door so no one could egress.

Synonyms: exit

_____
_____
_____
_____

Elaborate
(adj./v.) 1) very detailed or 2) to provide a detailed explanation

My teacher asked me to elaborate on my explanation.

Word family: elaboration
Synonyms: 1) detailed, complex; 2) explain

_____
_____
_____
_____

Directions:

Fill in the blanks using the words in the box. No word should be used more than once.

If you need help, first write the definition next to the vocab word in the box. Then find the best sentence for the word.

Deplorable	Derelict	Despair	Deteriorating	Discern	Dispute
	Dormant	Dreaded	Dubious	Elaborate	

1. Watching the sad movie filled me with _____ and made me cry.

2. The old abandoned house was dirty and _____.

3. When writing an essay, it's important to make sure you _____ on your argument.

4. The volcano wasn't threatening because it was _____.

5. I _____ taking my upcoming science test.

6. I think that lying and stealing are _____.

7. My sister said that she saw a mermaid, but I was _____ of what she saw.

8. If you're colorblind, it can be difficult to _____ the difference between the colors red and green.

9. My friend and I are in a _____. She thinks she is right, and I think I am right.

10. The veterinarian told us that my dog's health was _____, and I knew it would soon be time to say goodbye to my four-legged best friend.

Directions:
Select the best synonym for the vocabulary word.

1. Detain
    a. Desperate
    b. Delay
    c. Weaken
    d. Discredit

2. Detention
    a. Confinement
    b. Educational
    c. Punishment
    d. Thoroughfare

3. Detractor
    a. Believer
    b. Player
    c. Critic
    d. Empiricist

4. Dexterity
    a. Agility
    b. Fragility
    c. Incredulity
    d. Persnickety

5. Dignity
    a. Wonder
    b. Surprise
    c. Engraved
    d. Honor

6. Dilute
    a. Weaken
    b. Domineer
    c. Aspire
    d. Conspire

7. Dingy
    a. Mournful
    b. Important
    c. Dirty
    d. Desperate

8. Discredit
    a. Invalidate
    b. Credit
    c. Disdain
    d. Overlook

9. Disingenuous
    a. Ingenious
    b. Fake
    c. Fickle
    d. Weathered

10. Disparage
    a. Weep
    b. Criticize
    c. Whisper
    d. Shout

11. Disposition
    a. Temperament
    b. Action
    c. Latitude
    d. Audacity

12. Distort
    a. Twist
    b. Energize
    c. Criticize
    d. Smile

13. Dynamic
    a. Energetic
    b. Playful
    c. Proper
    d. Credible

14. Egoist
    a. Orator
    b. Educator
    c. Narcissist
    d. Simpleton

15. Egress
    a. Entrance
    b. Entryway
    c. Elegant
    d. Exit

Find the answer key for all sections on page 171

The Eighth Set: Elicit—Exacerbate

Directions: Read the vocab word card. Then write your own sentence using the vocab word.

Elicit
(v.) to draw or bring forth

My question didn't elicit a response from my grandma, who was watching TV.

Word family: elicitation
Synonyms: evoke

Elongate
(v.) to lengthen

A healthy lifestyle can elongate your life.

Synonyms: lengthen, extend

Emanate
(v.) 1) to spread 2) to originate

The warm air emanated from the kitchen, where my abuelita was baking.

Word family: emanating
Synonyms: emit, exude

Embargo
(n.) a ban, especially on trade

The United States put an embargo on trade with another country.

Synonyms: ban, restraint, barrier, stoppage

Embroider
(v.) 1) to sew a design on a piece of cloth 2) to make something more interesting by adding details that are untrue

My aunt has a habit of embroidering the truth when she tells a story.

Word family: embroidery
Synonyms: elaborate, embellish

Embryonic

(adj.) undeveloped

The idea was still embryonic.

Word family: embryo
Synonyms: rudimentary, beginning, initial

Empathetic

(adj.) having the ability to understand and share the feelings of others

I always try to be empathetic for people when they are having a bad day.

Word family: empathize, empathy
Synonyms: caring, understanding, sensitivity

Emulate

(v.) to copy or imitate

I always try to emulate my role models.

Word family: emulation
Synonyms: imitate, mirror

Enigma

(n.) mystery

Even to his friends, he was an enigma.

Word family: Enigmatic
Synonyms: mystery, puzzle

Ensue

(v.) to happen as a result

Chaos ensued when the wet dog ran into the living room.

Word family: ensuing
Synonyms: result, follow, arise

Entrepreneur

(n.) creative businessman

The entrepreneur's business idea was risky, but ultimately succesful.

Word family: entrepreneurial
Synonyms: businessperson

_____
_____
_____
_____

Epitomize

(v.) to be a perfect example

He epitomizes laziness.

Synonyms: exemplify, embody

_____
_____
_____
_____

Epoch

(n.) a large period of time

The Mesozoic Epoch is the scientific name for the period of time when dinosaurs lived.

Synonyms: era

_____
_____
_____
_____

Equate

(v.) to equal

In the past, one dollar equated to a lot more purchasing power. When she was little, my grandmother bought a beautiful toy for $5 that would be worth $50 today.

Word family: equation, equated, equal
Synonyms: correspond, connect, balance

_____
_____
_____
_____

Equivalent

(adj.) equal

1 + 1 is equivalent to 2.

Word family: equivalence
Synonyms: identical

_____
_____
_____

Era

(n.) a period of time (usually in the past)

Martin Luther King Jr. was a famous hero of the Civil Rights era.

Synonyms: epoch, period

Eradicate

(v.) to completely wipe out or destroy

The building manager tried to eradicate the mouse problem with mouse traps.

Word family: eradication
Synonyms: eliminate

Erode

(v.) to wear away

The soles of my sneakers eroded over time.

Word family: erosion
Synonyms: fade away

Erudite

(adj.) having or showing a lot of knowledge

The erudite student received the highest grades on her report card.

Synonyms: intellectual, knowledgeable, scholarly

Euphony

(n.) pleasant, harmonious sound

The euphony of the lullaby helped me fall asleep.

Word family: euphonic
Synonyms: melody

Euphoria

(n.) a feeling of great happiness or well-being

I felt euphoria when I found that my dad was coming home.

Word family: euphoric
Synonyms: bliss

_____
_____
_____
_____

Evacuate

(v). to leave or withdraw, as from a dangerous situation

The hurricane was so dangerous that the city was evacuated.

Word family: evacuation
Synonyms: remove

_____
_____
_____
_____

Evanescent

(adj.) lasting a short time, fading away gradually

Most flowers are evanescent, blooming in the spring and wilting in the fall.

Word family: evanescence
Synonyms: fleeting, fading

_____
_____
_____
_____

Evoke

(v.) to bring up

Superhero movies evoke feelings of excitement and adventure.

Word family: evocation, evocative
Synonyms: elicit, stir

_____
_____
_____

Exacerbate

(v.) to make worse

His rude comments exacerbated the tensions in the room.

Word family: exacerbation
Synonyms: aggravate

_____
_____
_____

Directions:

Fill in the blanks using the words in the box. No word should be used more than once.

If you need help, first write the definition next to the vocab word in the box. Then find the best sentence for the word.

Elicit	Emanated	Embroidered	Empathetic	Entrepreneur	Equates

Era   Eradicate   Euphony   Evacuate

1. Heat _____ off the sidewalk in the summer.

2. A funny joke can _____ a lot of laughter.

3. The orchestra produced a beautiful _____.

4. The _____ founded a new and succesful company.

5. During the hurricane, all of my family and friends needed to _____ the

    city.

6. In order to _____ world hunger, we need to make sure everyone has

    ongoing access to healthy food.

7. The Renaissance was an _____ of history where people began to spend more

    time engaging in the arts and education.

8. I took my sewing needle and _____ my initials into my jacket.

9. A dark storm cloud usually _____ to an incoming storm.

10. My grandfather is the most _____ person I know. He always knows when

    someone is feeling sad and what to do to cheer them up.

Directions:

Select the best synonym for the vocabulary word.

1. Elongate
    a. Extend
    b. Shorten
    c. Limited
    d. Arising

2. Embargo
    a. Barrage
    b. Ban
    c. Float
    d. Adamant

3. Embryonic
    a. Rancid
    b. Embittered
    c. Clear
    d. Rudimentary

4. Emulate
    a. Benign
    b. Weary
    c. Imitate
    d. Luminous

5. Enigma
    a. Mystery
    b. Eloquent
    c. Aspirational
    d. Dingy

6. Ensue
    a. Berate
    b. Briny
    c. Arise
    d. Demure

7. Epitomize
    a. Embody
    b. Bewilder
    c. Share
    d. Patronize

8. Epoch
    a. Epic
    b. Damage
    c. Joyful
    d. Era

9. Equivalent
    a. Identical
    b. Deficient
    c. According
    d. Obedience

10. Erode
    a. Contend
    b. Fade
    c. Eradicate
    d. Grow

11. Erudite
    a. Joyful
    b. Assiduous
    c. Scholarly
    d. Genuine

12. Euphoria
    a. Bliss
    b. Pleasing Sounds
    c. Order
    d. Cacophony

13. Evanescent
    a. Industrious
    b. Autonomy
    c. Fleeting
    d. Interpretation

14. Evoke
    a. Comprehend
    b. Elicit
    c. Disparage
    d. Grow

15. Exacerbate
    a. Punish
    b. Worsen
    c. Excite
    d. Appraise

Find the answer key for all sections on page 171

The Ninth Set: Exasperate—Fusion

Directions: Read the vocab word card. Then write your own sentence using the vocab word.

Exasperate

(v.) to make very angry or impatient

My sister exasperates me when she takes my clothes.

Word family: exasperated, exasperation
Synonyms: infuriate, annoy

_____

_____

_____

_____

Excavate

(v.) to dig up

The treasure hunters used shovels to excavate the buried treasure.

Word family: excavation
Synonyms: dig

_____

_____

_____

_____

Exclusion

(n.) not being allowed to enter or join

After I got into a fight with my friend, I was excluded from his birthday party.

Word family: exclude, excluded
Synonyms: banishment; ban, bar

_____

_____

_____

_____

Exile

(v.) to banish someone from their native country

He was banished from the country and was never allowed to return.

Synonyms: banish

_____

_____

_____

_____

Exquisite

(adj.) beautifully made or designed

Her quinceañera dress was exquisite.

Synonyms: beautiful, elegant

_____

_____

_____

_____

Extinct

(adj.) no longer existing

The dodo bird became extinct in 1681.

Word family: extinction
Synonyms: vanished, dead

_____

_____

_____

_____

Extol

(v.) to praise

The teacher was extolled for his caring and helpful teaching style.

Synonyms: exalt

_____

_____

_____

_____

Exuberant

(adj.) overflowing with joy or happiness

My new puppy was exuberantly jumping up and down.

Word family: exuberance, exuberantly
Synonyms: ebullient, cheerful

_____

_____

_____

_____

Fabricate

(v.) 1) to lie, to make up, to invent; 2) to manufacturer

My parents told me not to fabricate the truth.

Word family: fabrication
Synonyms: make up, fake

_____

_____

_____

_____

Facet

(n.) an aspect of something

One facet of the game plan involved me faking out the other player.

Synonyms: aspect, feature, dimension

_____

_____

_____

_____

Fallacy

(n.) a false or mistaken idea

Some people believe that money can buy happiness, others believe it is a fallacy.

Synonyms: misconception, misbelief, falsehood

Fathom

(v.) to understand

He couldn't fathom why she was so mad at him.

Synonyms: comprehend

Feasible

(adj.) possible, able to be done

It isn't feasible to swim the Atlantic Ocean in one day.

Word family: feasibility
Synonyms: possible, practical, believable, do-able

Felicity

(n.) joy and happiness

The holidays are a time of great felicity for my family.

Word family: felicitations
Synonyms: bliss, delight

Feral

(adj.) wild and untamed

Feral cats must survive by catching small animals or scavenging food.

Synonyms: undomesticated

Fission

(n.) a splitting apart

The company's fission meant there were now 2 companies instead of 1.

Synonyms: division, splitting

Flamboyant

(adj.) over the top

The red sports car was the most flamboyant car in the parking lot.

Word family: flamboyance
Synonyms: ostentatious

Fluctuate

(v.) to shift back and forth without regularity

The temperatures in the desert can fluctuate from very hot in the day to very cold at night.

Word family: fluctuation
Synonyms: vary, differ, waver

Foment

(v.) try to stir up public opinion

His speeches fomented public displeasure, resulting in many protests.

Word family: fomentation
Synonyms: incite

Founder

(v.) 1) to sink; 2) someone who starts a company

The boat began to founder.

Synonyms: 1) sink or 2) entrepreneur

Frank

(adj.) honest and open

Can we please have a frank discussion?

Word family: frankness
Synonyms: candid

_____

_____

_____

_____

Fringe

(n). the edge or outer portion

Alicia is on the fringe of my friend group. We hang out sometimes, but not often.

Synonyms: peripheral

_____

_____

_____

_____

Frugal

(adj.) not wasteful or extravagant

If you want to save money, you need to be frugal.

Word family: frugality
Synonyms: thrifty

_____

_____

_____

_____

Fundamental

(adj.) essential

All humans have the fundamental right to clean drinking water.

Synonyms: basic

_____

_____

_____

_____

Fusion

(v.) a joining together

The fusion of the two soccer teams into one team meant that there were now two goalies instead of one.

Word family: fuse
Synonyms: blend, merging

_____

_____

_____

_____

Directions:

Fill in the blanks using the words in the box. No word should be used more than once.

If you need help, first write the definition next to the vocab word in the box. Then find the best sentence for the word.

Excavate	Exquisite	Extinct	Exuberant	Fathom	Feasible
	Fluctuate	Frank	Frugal	Fundamental	

1. In the spring, temperatures can _____ from really cold to very warm.

2. Scientists found a fossil of a dinosaur that they needed to _____ from the ground using hammers and shovels.

3. I decided to be _____ and tell my sister the truth.

4. Dinosaurs are _____. The last dinosaur died thousands of years ago.

5. On my birthday, I am always _____ because I love getting gifts and eating my birthday cake.

6. If you want to save your money, you need to be a _____ spender.

7. I cannot _____ why my teacher gave us 500 pages of reading for homework.

8. My sister's dress was so _____. It was colorful and detailed with many little diamonds.

9. Eating food and drinking clean water is _____ for human life.

10. I wanted to play football with my friends. However, it started to snow and playing football in the snow isn't really _____.

Directions:

Select the best synonym for the vocabulary word.

1. Exasperate
    a. Annoy
    b. Worsen
    c. Allege
    d. Improve

2. Exclusion
    a. Include
    b. Ban
    c. Deceit
    d. Communication

3. Exile
    a. Banish
    b. Vague
    c. Scold
    d. Aggravate

4. Extol
    a. Praise
    b. Decide
    c. Afflict
    d. Affect

5. Fabricate
    a. Worsen
    b. Embroider
    c. Shape
    d. Surrender

6. Facet
    a. Truth
    b. Aspect
    c. Menace
    d. Spiked

7. Fallacy
    a. Falsehood
    b. Indecisive
    c. Hostility
    d. Criticality

8. Felicity
    a. Bliss
    b. Nobility
    c. Wild
    d. Escapade

9. Feral
    a. Wild
    b. Sharp
    c. Shapeless
    d. Ancient

10. Fission
    a. Boldness
    b. Accomplishment
    c. Merge
    d. Divide

11. Flamboyant
    a. Calamitous
    b. Befuddlement
    c. Ostentatious
    d. Caution

12. Foment
    a. Tragedy
    b. Embarrassment
    c. Incite
    d. Insight

13. Founder
    a. Schism
    b. Sink
    c. Rift
    d. Fickle

14. Fringe
    a. Inconstant
    b. Periphery
    c. Burly
    d. Truthful

15. Fusion
    a. Merge
    b. Divide
    c. Advantage
    d. Browbeat

Find the answer key for all sections on page 171

The Tenth Set: Garrulous—Implicate

Directions: Read the vocab word card. Then write your own sentence using the vocab word.

Garrulous
(adj.) talkative

My most garrulous friend can talk for hours.

Synonyms: loquacious

_____

_____

_____

_____

Gaunt
(adj.) very thin or bony

The doctor was worried about the health of her gaunt patient.

Synonyms: skinny, bony, haggard

_____

_____

_____

_____

Genre
(n.) a specific style of art or literature

My favorite genre to read is mystery or sports fiction.

Synonyms: type, kind

_____

_____

_____

_____

Gingerly
(adv.) carefully

She walked gingerly across the tightrope.

Synonyms: cautiously, with care

_____

_____

_____

_____

Glutton
(n.) one who eats and drinks too much, greedy

When it came to dessert, I was a total glutton.

Word family: gluttonous
Synonyms: greedy, insatiable

_____

_____

_____

_____

Grandeur
(n.) grand elegance

The grandeur of the palace was breathtaking.

Word family: grand
Synonyms: splendor

_____

_____

_____

_____

Gregarious
(adj.) outgoing and social

I can be very gregarious at parties.

Word family: gregariousness
Synonyms: sociable

_____

_____

_____

_____

Grimace
(n.) a facial expression of fear or disapproval

Her mom grimaced when Laila told her about the bad grade in math.

Synonyms: frown, wince, scowl

_____

_____

_____

_____

Grovel
(v.) to beg

I groveled at my parent's feet, hoping they would take pity on me and let me go to the amusement park with the rest of my classmates.

Synonyms: beg

_____

_____

_____

_____

Hackneyed
(adj.) overused and old-fashioned

I think that most knock-knock jokes are hackneyed and not funny.

Synonyms: overdone, worn out

_____

_____

_____

_____

Hasty

(adj.) rushed, sloppy, very quick

Don't make hasty decisions about important life choices.

Word family: haste
Synonyms: hurried

_____

_____

_____

_____

Hilarity

(n.) amusement

My family all laughed in hilarity at my uncle's funny joke.

Word family: hilarious
Synonyms: mirth, merriment

_____

_____

_____

_____

Hoary

(adj.) 1) very old; 2) gray from old age

Over time, the fabric became hoary with age.

Synonyms: hackneyed, banal, old

_____

_____

_____

_____

Hovel

(n.) a small, unpleasant building or room

On the edge of town, there was an abandoned hovel.

Synonyms: shack

_____

_____

_____

_____

Hue

(n.) the color or shade of an object

My favorite hue of green is lime green.

Synonyms: shade

_____

_____

_____

Idiosyncrasy

(n.) a characteristic peculiar to an individual

My friend has an idiosyncrasy where every time she laughs, she snorts.

Word family: idiosyncratic
Synonyms: quirk, peculiarity

Ignoble

(adj.) dishonorable, shameful

The villain of the story was ignoble.

Synonyms: shameful, contemptible

Illuminate

(v.) to light up or to make clear

The moon illuminated the night sky.

Word family: illumination, luminous, luminary
Synonyms: light up or illustrate

Immaculate

(adj.) perfectly clean

I always keep my bedroom immaculate, but my sister is very messy.

Synonyms: spotless, pristine

Impasse

(n.) a deadlock, a point at which one can go no

We couldn't agree on what to eat for dinner. We were at an impasse.

Synonyms: standstill

Impediment
(n.) an obstacle, something in the way

Being afraid of change is an impediment to growing and learning.

Word family: impede
Synonyms: obstruction

Imperial
(adj). like royalty

The imperial palace was filled with gold furniture.

Word family: imperialist
Synonyms: royal, regal

Imperious
(adj.) arrogant, behaving like royalty

My boss sometimes speaks to me in an imperious tone.

Synonyms: commanding, overbearing

Impervious
(adj.) 1) unable to pass or enter; 2) unable to upset

Even though my little brother tries to annoy me, I am impervious to his childish behavior and pranks.

Synonyms: impermeable, impenetrable

Implicate
(v.) to involve in, to connect with, or be related to

The criminal was implicated in the crime.

Word family: implication, imply
Synonyms: involvement, connection

Directions:

Fill in the blanks using the words in the box. No word should be used more than once.

If you need help, first write the definition next to the vocab word in the box. Then find the best sentence for the word.

Garrulous	Gingerly	Glutton	Grimace	Groveling	Hasty
	Hue	Illuminated	Impasse	Imperial	

1. The sky was a beautiful _____ of blue.

2. When the fire alarm went off, my teacher instructed the class to walk _____ to

   the exit.

3. The bright light _____ the room.

4. The _____ palace, where the Queen lived, was beautiful.

5. My dad is really _____. He talks to everyone and anyone at parties.

6. When my sister was deciding what college to go to, my mom told her to take her time and not to

   make any _____ decisions.

7. When it comes to chocolate, I am a _____. I could eat chocolate for

   breakfast, lunch, and dinner.

8. Even after talking about it for an hour, my family couldn't agree on what to eat for dinner. We

   were at an _____.

9. I tried to convince my parents to let me go to my friend's house by _____.

10. The _____ on my grandma's face is a tell-tale sign that she is very angry.

Directions:

Select the best synonym for the vocabulary word.

1. Gaunt
   a. Belittle
   b. Thin
   c. Deception
   d. Timid

2. Genre
   a. Type
   b. Debate
   c. Exist
   d. Era

3. Grandeur
   a. Illumination
   b. Splendor
   c. Audible
   d. Dynamic

4. Gregarious
   a. Guidance
   b. Burgeon
   c. Adept
   d. Sociable

5. Hackneyed
   a. Regrettable
   b. Dereliction
   c. Hoary
   d. Politeness

6. Hilarity
   a. Merriment
   b. Hysterics
   c. Chaotic
   d. Capability

7. Hoary
   a. Old
   b. Geniality
   c. Scorn
   d. Adjacent

8. Hovel
   a. Shack
   b. Obey
   c. Authorize
   d. Diligent

9. Idiosyncrasy
   a. Account
   b. Peculiarity
   c. Patronize
   d. Inclusivity

10. Ignoble
    a. Exhausting
    b. Conscious
    c. Contemptible
    d. Adequate

11. Immaculate
    a. Chasm
    b. Prejudice
    c. Contradictory
    d. Spotless

12. Impediment
    a. Authentic
    b. Baleful
    c. Obstruction
    d. Barbed

13. Imperious
    a. Evanescent
    b. Cheerful
    c. Domesticated
    d. Commanding

14. Impervious
    a. Gingerly
    b. Frugal
    c. Impermeable
    d. Loquacious

15. Implicate
    a. Fluctuate
    b. Involve
    c. Scowl
    d. Extend

Find the answer key for all sections on page 171

The Eleventh Set: Implore—Intricate

Directions: Read the vocab word card. Then write your own sentence using the vocab word.

Implore
(v.) to beg or ask earnestly

I implore you to reconsider your decision.

Synonyms: ask, beg

_____

_____

_____

_____

Imply
(v.) to express indirectly

Her words implied she was angry, even though she didn't directly say so.

Word family: implication
Synonyms: suggest

_____

_____

_____

Inarticulate
(adj.) unable to speak or express clearly

I was so angry that I was inarticulate when I tried to argue back with my parents.

Synonyms: tongue-tied, unclear

_____

_____

_____

Inclination
(n.) preference or tendency

Because of my sweet tooth, I have a natural inclination for dessert before dinner.

Word family: inclined
Synonyms: tendency

_____

_____

_____

_____

Incompetent
(adj.) not able to do something properly

I'm incompetent at tennis.

Word family: incompetence, competent, competence
Synonyms: inept, unskilled

_____

_____

_____

Incumbent

(n./adj.) 1) someone who is currently holding a political position; 2) necessary

The incumbent senator was running against a new, much younger politician.

Synonyms: 1) office-holder 2) necessary

Indictment

(n.) a charge or accusation of a serious crime

The grand jury's indictment meant that Eleanor would need to go to court and get a lawyer.

Word family: indict
Synonyms: charge, accusation

Indifferent

(adj.) having no particular interest in something

She was angry at her classmates for being so indifferent to climate change.

Synonyms: unconcerned

Indignant

(adj.) feeling angry or insulted from an injustice

When my baby brother doesn't get his way, he can be indignant.

Synonyms: resentful, disgruntled, discontented

Inevitable

(adj.) certain to happen

Death is inevitable for all humans.

Word family: inevitability
Synonyms: unavoidable

Infamous

(adj.) being famous for a bad reason; having a bad reputation

Bonnie and Clyde were the most infamous criminals of their time.

Synonyms: notorious, scandalous

Ingenuous

(adj.) innocent, sincere, naïve

The young man had never spent time outside of his privileged life and was therefore quite ingenuous.

Word family: disingenuous
Synonyms: innocent, trusting

Ingenuity

(n.) innovation, creativity

The inventor was known for her ingenuity.

Word family: ingenious
Synonyms: inventiveness, creativity

Innate

(adj.) born with, not learned

I was born with an innate talent for making people laugh.

Synonyms: natural

Innovative

(adj.) introducing something new, creative

At the time, the technology was quite innovative.

Word family: innovate, innovation
Synonyms: ingenious, novel, original, creative

Inquiry

(n.) a question or request for information

Her inquiry into animal cloning eventually led to the first ever cloned sheep.

Word family: inquire, inquiring
Synonyms: question, investigation

Inscribe

(v.) to write or etch words on or into a surface

I had my initials inscribed on my bracelet.

Word family: scribe, inscription
Synonyms: write, carve, etch, engrave

Insinuation

(n.) a sneaky suggestion of something bad

I was offended by the insinuation that I had cheated on the test.

Word family: insinuate
Synonyms: suggestion, hint

Insipid

(adj.) boring or tasteless

The music was so insipid that I began to fall asleep.

Synonyms: uninteresting, dull, flavorless

Insolent

(adj.) rude, disrespectful

My little sister can be very insolent when she doesn't get her way.

Synonyms: impertinent, impudent

Intangible

(adj.) not able to be touched or sensed; impossible to understand

Love is intangible. You can't touch it, but that doesn't mean it's not real.

Word family: tangible, tangibility
Synonyms: untouchable, not physical

_____
_____
_____
_____
_____

Integrate

(v). to bring together

In 1955, the school board voted to integrate a previously all-white school, which led to the courageous attendance of nine Black students.

Word family: integration, integrative
Synonyms: combine, merge

_____
_____
_____
_____

Integrity

(n.) a person's moral character

People with integrity tell the truth.

Synonyms: honesty, honor

_____
_____
_____
_____

Intrepid

(adj.) fearless, adventurous

In 1955, Rosa Parks made the intrepid decision to not give her up her seat on a bus to a white passenger.

Word family: trepid, trepidation
Synonyms: fearless, brave, courageous

_____
_____
_____
_____

Intricate

(adj.) complex

The ceiling of the Sistine Chapel is painted with an intricate design.

Word family: intricately
Synonyms: complicated, very detailed

_____
_____
_____

Directions:

Fill in the blanks using the words in the box. No word should be used more than once.

If you need help, first write the definition next to the vocab word in the box. Then find the best sentence for the word.

Incompetent	Indifferent	Inevitable	Infamous	Innovative
Insolent	Intrepid	Integrity	Intangible	Intricate

1. It's important to do the right thing and act with _____.

2. Happiness is _____; you can't touch happiness or hold it in your hands.

3. Sometimes I feel _____ in my social studies class because I don't know many dates or historical facts.

4. Bonnie and Clyde are two of history's most _____ criminals

5. The telephone is an example of an _____ invention that changed the world.

6. In class, we read a book with a very _____ plot. It had so many plot twists and characters that it was sometimes difficult to understand what was happening.

7. When it comes to choosing between pizza and pasta, I am _____. I don't care which we eat for dinner because I like both.

8. Most of my role models are _____ people who never give up even in the face of danger.

9. My little brother can be _____ when he doesn't get what he wants.

10. The sun always rises in the east and sets in the sun. It is _____.

Directions:

Select the best synonym for the vocabulary word.

1. Implore
   a. Stimulate
   b. Beg
   c. Resent
   d. Question

2. Imply
   a. Obstruct
   b. Involve
   c. Suggest
   d. Tendency

3. Inarticulate
   a. Ill-expressed
   b. Resent
   c. Scandalous
   d. Ingenious

4. Inclination
   a. Tendency
   b. Burden
   c. Contestation
   d. Periphery

5. Incumbent
   a. Overdone
   b. Scowl
   c. Glutton
   d. Office-holder

6. Indictment
   a. Misconception
   b. Flamboyance
   c. Accusation
   d. Bliss

7. Indignant
   a. Discontent
   b. Embryonic
   c. Varnish
   d. Ebullience

8. Ingenuous
   a. Rudimentary
   b. Insightful
   c. Trusting
   d. Identical

9. Ingenuity
   a. Innovative
   b. Dismal
   c. Invalidate
   d. Belittlement

10. Innate
    a. Dismal
    b. Edict
    c. Detain
    d. Natural

11. Inquiry
    a. Investigation
    b. Guidance
    c. Command
    d. Opposition

12. Inscribe
    a. Expose
    b. Weaken
    c. Dig
    d. Engrave

13. Insinuation
    a. Implication
    b. Patronize
    c. Obedience
    d. Communal

14. Insipid
    a. Prudent
    b. Truthful
    c. Boring
    d. Covert

15. Integrate
    a. Aggravate
    b. Torment
    c. Merge
    d. Increase

Find the answer key for all sections on page 171

The Twelfth Set: Invigorate—Livid

Directions: Read the vocab word card. Then write your own sentence using the vocab word.

Invigorate
(v.) to fill with strength and energy

I felt invigorated after a good meal and a hot shower.

Word family: vigor
Synonyms: energize, revive, revitalize

_____
_____
_____
_____

Irate
(adj.) very angry

My parents were irate when I crashed their car.

Synonyms: furious

_____
_____
_____
_____

Ironic
(adj.) saying one thing, but meaning the opposite, sometimes as a form of humor

I played the same many times, my mom said "Wow, I love listening to one song 5 times in a row." I knew she was being ironic.

Word family: irony
Synonyms: sarcastic

_____
_____
_____
_____

Irrefutable
(adj.) impossible to deny

It is an irrefutable fact that humans need oxygen.

Word family: refute
Synonyms: undeniable

_____
_____
_____
_____

Irreverent
(adj.) disrespectful

The newspaper's irreverent portrayal of the politician made him angry.

Word family: irreverence
Synonyms: scornful, disdainful

_____
_____
_____
_____

Itinerant

(adj.) nomadic, constantly moving

Professional athletes live itinerant lifestyles, flying all over the world to play games.

Word family: itinerary
Synonyms: transient, nomadic

Jargon

(n.) the specialized language or vocabulary

Medical jargon can be hard to understand unless you've attended medical school.

Synonyms: lingo, language

Jeer

(v.) to make fun of or insult someone

She tried to ignore the jeering crowd.

Word family: jeering
Synonyms: mock, taunt, ridicule

Jest

(v.) to joke

The jest was not very funny.

Word family: jester
Synonyms: joke

Jubilant

(adj.) overly joyful

The jubilant celebration was filled with dancing and laughter.

Word family: jubilance, jubilation
Synonyms: exultant, joyful

Juxtapose

(v.) contrasting two very different things

The sun in the sky juxtaposed the sadness of the funeral happening that day.

Word family: juxtaposition
Synonyms: compare, contrast

Keen

(adj.) sharp-witted and intelligent

She was a keen businesswoman who made a lot of money from her business decisions.

Synonyms: sharp, observant, perceptive

Kinetic

(adj.) moving

Some students may be kinetic learners, who learn better when their body is allowed to move during lessons.

Word family: kinesthetic
Synonyms: dynamic, energized

Laden

(adj.) weighed down with a large amount of something, burdensome

Foods that are laden with sugar are bad for you.

Synonyms: loaded, burdened

Lament

(v.) to express grief, to mourn

At the time, the technology was quite innovative.

Word family: lamenting, lamentation
Synonyms: groan, weep, mourn

Languid

(adj.) slow-moving

Sloths may be the most languid animal in the animal kingdom.

Word family: languorous
Synonyms: relaxed, slow, unenergetic

_____

Laud

(v.) to praise

She was lauded for her kindness.

Word family: laudatory
Synonyms: extol, exalt

_____

Laudatory

(adj.) expressing praise

The movie received laudatory reviews from film critics.

Word family: laud
Synonyms: praising, extolling

_____

Lavish

(adj.) extravagant; spending a lot or giving a lot

On Valentine's Day, he gave her a lavish display of red roses.

Synonyms: luxurious, grand, expensive

_____

Lax

(adj.) careless

The museum had lax security, so we were able to slip past the guards and enjoy a free day at the museum.

Word family: relax, lackadaisical
Synonyms: lazy

Leach
(v.) to wash or dissolve away

The water leached away all the hairspray from my hair.

Synonyms: drain

Leer
(n). a look or gaze in an unpleasant or malicious way

I looked away from her leering face.

Word family: leering, leeringly
Synonyms: ogle

Lenient
(adj.) tolerant, merciful, generous

I prefer my lenient teacher over my strict teacher.

Word family: leniently
Synonyms: forgiving, relaxed

Linger
(v.) to delay or be slow in leaving

The smell of burnt toast lingered even after we'd cleaned out the toaster.

Word family: lingering
Synonyms: remain, continue, stay

Livid
(adj.) discolored, bruised, or very angry

My parents were livid about my bad grade.

Synonyms: enraged, furious

Directions:

Fill in the blanks using the words in the box. No word should be used more than once.

If you need help, first write the definition next to the vocab word in the box. Then find the best sentence for the word.

Invigorated	Irate	Jargon	Jests	Jubilant	Lamented
	Lauded	Lavish	Lenient	Linger	

1. A lot of doctors speak in medical _____, which can make it difficult to understand them.

2. I was so _____ when I found out my chess tournament was cancelled. I had practiced so hard and I had been so excited to participate.

3. My best friend is very funny and is always making people laugh with her _____.

4. At the end of the school day, most of my friends _____ in the hallway so we can talk and make plans for the weekend.

5. My math teacher is very _____. She doesn't get mad at us for talking in class and doesn't give us consequences for being late to class.

6. I was _____ on the day of my graduation. I was so excited and proud to cross the stage and get my diploma.

7. I always feel _____ after a good sleep and a health breakfast.

8. I _____ the death of my favorite goldfish, Marigold.

9. Garrett Morgan is a famous inventor, who is _____ for such inventions as the traffic signal.

10. The President always hosts a number of _____ parties on Inauguration day, filled with good food, good music, and many famous celebrities.

Directions:
Select the best synonym for the vocabulary word.

1. Ironic
   a. Sarcastic
   b. Forgiving
   c. Undeniable
   d. Transient

2. Irrefutable
   a. Ingenious
   b. Undeniable
   c. Untouchable
   d. Exhausted

3. Irreverent
   a. Sympathetic
   b. Pleasant
   c. Notorious
   d. Scornful

4. Itinerant
   a. Transient
   b. Original
   c. Honest
   d. Intrepid

5. Jeer
   a. Scowl
   b. Trust
   c. Beg
   d. Taunt

6. Juxtapose
   a. Contrast
   b. Suggest
   c. Impose
   d. Enforce

7. Keen
   a. Observant
   b. Inept
   c. Impudent
   d. Prudent

8. Kinetic
   a. Willful
   b. Dynamic
   c. Sociable
   d. Captious

9. Laden
   a. Impermeable
   b. Burdened
   c. Splendid
   d. Haggard

10. Languid
    a. Garrulous
    b. Thrifty
    c. Delighted
    d. Relaxed

11. Laudatory
    a. Celebrated
    b. Domesticated
    c. Cheerful
    d. Elegant

12. Lax
    a. Gaunt
    b. Relaxed
    c. Artificial
    d. Fleeting

13. Leach
    a. Drain
    b. Epoch
    c. Exemplify
    d. Aggravate

14. Leer
    a. Whisper
    b. Ogle
    c. Fear
    d. Evoke

15. Livid
    a. Peruse
    b. Placate
    c. Irate
    d. Pertain

Find the answer key for all sections on page 171

The Thirteenth Set: Locomotion—Objective

Directions: Read the vocab word card. Then write your own sentence using the vocab word.

Locomotion
(n.) motion

Running is one form of locomotion.

Word family: locomotor, locomote
Synonyms: movement

_____

_____

_____

_____

Loquacious
(adj.) talkative

Talk show hosts tend to be very loquacious people.

Synonyms: garrulous, talkative

_____

_____

_____

_____

Lush
(adj.) full of plant life

The lush jungle was filled with the sounds of birds and other animals.

Synonyms: abundant

_____

_____

_____

_____

Maladroit
(adj.) clumsy

I was such a maladroit player that I spent most of the season sitting on the bench.

Synonyms: awkward, incompetent

_____

_____

_____

_____

Malevolence
(n.) meanness or hatred

His Aunt Jenna's malevolence made him dislike her so much that he faked a cold so he wouldn't need to visit her.

Word family: malevolent
Synonyms: meanness, hatred, badness

_____

_____

_____

_____

Mar

(v.) to ruin

The accident marred his hand, leaving him with a lifelong scar.

Synonyms: spoil

Mercurial

(adj.) characterized by rapid and unpredictable change

Her mercurial personality was difficult to be around. Her moods changed so fast that no one could keep up.

Synonyms: volatile, capricious, temperamental

Merge

(v.) to blend together

The two soccer teams decided to merge, so now there were two goalies and too many people sitting on the bench.

Word family: merger, merging
Synonyms: combine, blend, integrate

Meticulous

(adj.) careful, paying attention to details

When it comes to my homework, I am always meticulous. It seems silly to lose points on something so easy.

Synonyms: conscientious, immaculate

Mirth

(n.) happiness and good cheer

The holidays are a time filled with mirth and joyous laughter for my family.

Synonyms: cheerfulness, merriment

Misconstrue
(v.) misinterpret

Don't misconstrue my words. That's not what I meant.

Word family: construe
Synonyms: misunderstand

Miserly
(adj.) cheap

Ebenezer Scrooge was a miserly old man who didn't like to spend any of his wealth.

Word family: miser
Synonyms: frugal, thrifty

Mitigate
(v.) to make less severe, to moderate, to lessen the effect of something

I was able to mitigate my parent's anger by promising to do my homework every day for the rest of the year.

Synonyms: alleviate, reduce, diminish

Molten
(adj.) melted

Molten lava poured down the active volcano.

Synonyms: liquid

Monotonous
(adj.) boring

The teacher's monotonous voice put Aaron to sleep.

Word family: monotone
Synonyms: tedious, dull, unexciting

Nautical
(adj.) related to sailing or the sea

The sailor was a nautical genius. She could sail through any kind of weather without a compass or map.

Synonyms: naval, maritime, seagoing

_____

_____

_____

_____

Nimble
(adj.) agile and flexible

Sewing requires nimble fingers.

Word family: nimbleness
Synonyms: lithe, quick

_____

_____

_____

Nonchalant
(adj.) without concern

She was surprisingly nonchalant about winning the impressive award.

Synonyms: calm, cool, unconcerned

_____

_____

_____

_____

Notorious
(adj.) known widely and unfavorably

The teacher was notoriously strict.

Synonyms: infamous

_____

_____

_____

_____

Novice
(n.) a beginner

All expert chess players were once novice players.

Synonyms: amateur

_____

_____

_____

_____

Noxious

(adj.) harmful, poisonous

Some plants are noxious for humans.

Synonyms: toxic

_____
_____
_____
_____

Null

(adj). of zero value, nothing

If the contract wasn't signed by both people within five days, it became null.

Word family: nullify, annul, annulment
Synonyms: void, invalid

_____
_____
_____
_____

Nullify

(v.) to make of something "zero" or to cancel the effect of something

An antidote can nullify the effect of a poison.

Word family: null, annul, annulment
Synonyms: void, invalidate

_____
_____
_____
_____

Obdurate

(adj.) stubborn

He was the most obdurate person I know. He always believed he was right.

Synonyms: adamant, obstinate

_____
_____
_____
_____

Objective

(adj.) not influenced by personal opinion

It can be hard to be objective when your two friends are fighting.

Synonyms: unbiased, nonpartisan

_____
_____
_____
_____

Directions:

Fill in the blanks using the words in the box. No word should be used more than once.

If you need help, first write the definition next to the vocab word in the box. Then find the best sentence for the word.

Loquacious	Malevolence	Marred	Meticulous	Mirth
Nautical	Novice	Noxious	Nullify	Obdurate

1. I decided to have a _____-themed party. We had a cake the shape of a sailboat, and sailing-themed games.

2. You are a _____ before you become a master chess player. But this takes years and a lot of practice.

3. The car crash _____ the car with a big dent and many scratches.

4. I like when my room is _____, so I always make my bed and clean up the floor.

5. My step-mom is very _____. She can talk for hours to anyone she meets.

6. The hero of a story is usually courageous and kind, whereas you can usually recognize the villain by their _____.

7. I love parties because they're usually filled with _____, good music, and friends.

8. I knew the plant was poisonous because it had a particularly _____ smell.

9. My brother is very _____. He cries and yells when he doesn't get his way.

10. I took an antidote to _____ the effect of the poison.

Directions:

Select the best synonym for the vocabulary word.

1. Locomotion
   a. Movement
   b. Amateur
   c. Laudatory
   d. Admiring

2. Lush
   a. Young
   b. Lucrative
   c. Emboldened
   d. Abundant

3. Maladroit
   a. Capricious
   b. Clumsy
   c. Characterized
   d. Capital

4. Mercurial
   a. Volatile
   b. Garrulous
   c. Enraged
   d. Merry

5. Merge
   a. Whimper
   b. Falter
   c. Coalesce
   d. Illuminate

6. Misconstrue
   a. Dilute
   b. Suspect
   c. Misinterpret
   d. Rudimentary

7. Miserly
   a. Cheap
   b. Extravagant
   c. Ostentatious
   d. Old-fashioned

8. Mitigate
   a. Mirror
   b. Embody
   c. Alleviate
   d. Puzzle

9. Molten
   a. Sorrow
   b. Melted
   c. Excavated
   d. Melodic

10. Monotonous
    a. Restful
    b. Belittled
    c. Tedious
    d. Pristine

11. Nimble
    a. Lithe
    b. Unconcerned
    c. Spotless
    d. Royal

12. Nonchalant
    a. Isolated
    b. Invulnerable
    c. Calm
    d. Lonely

13. Notorious
    a. Infamous
    b. Hopeless
    c. Dismal
    d. Adept

14. Null
    a. Wrong
    b. Notorious
    c. Disparate
    d. Void

15. Objective
    a. Suspicious
    b. Unbiased
    c. Biased
    d. Subjective

Find the answer key for all sections on page 171

The Fourteenth Set: Obscure—Pernicious

Directions: Read the vocab word card. Then write your own sentence using the vocab word.

Obscure
(adj.) hidden; hard to see or understand

Some math concepts seem really obscure at first, but once you practice them, they get easier to understand.

Synonyms: unclear, hidden

_____

_____

_____

_____

Obsolete
(adj.) out of date, no longer useful

Horse-drawn carriages are pretty much obsolete in the 21st century.

Synonyms: old fashioned, outdated

_____

_____

_____

_____

Obstinate
(adj.) stubborn

Carlisle is my most obstinate friend. He will only play games that he wants to.

Synonyms: adamant, obdurate

_____

_____

_____

_____

Obstruction
(n.) a barrier or obstacle

The tree in the middle of the road was an obstruction that created hours of traffic.

Word family: obstruct
Synonyms: impediment

_____

_____

_____

_____

Ominous
(adj.) threatening or foreshadowing something bad

The storm clouds in the distance looked ominous.

Word family: omen
Synonyms: threatening, baleful, menacing, sinister

_____

_____

_____

_____

Opaque

(adj.) impossible to see through, preventing the passage of light

The opaque blinds helped to keep the morning sun out of the room so Jesse could sleep longer.

Word family: opacity
Synonyms: cloudy, nontransparent

Open-handed

(adj.) generous

Andrew Carnegie was known to be an open-handed businessman, who gave money away to many various charities.

Synonyms: charitable, benevolent

Opulent

(adj.) rich, characterized by wealth

The palace was filled with opulent decorations and grand furniture.

Word family: opulence
Synonyms: wealthy, lavish

Oration

(n.) a formal speech

One of Martin Luther King Jr.'s most famous orations was his "I had a dream" speech.

Word family: orate, orator
Synonyms: speech

Orator

(n.) public speaker

Martin Luther King Jr. was a famous orator.

Word family: orate, oration
Synonyms: rhetorician, public speaker

Ostentatious
(adj.) showy, pretentious

The most ostentatious car in the parking lot is a little red convertible.

Synonyms: flamboyant, extravagant

Pact
(n.) a formal agreement between two countries

They made a pact to always be friends.

Synonyms: agreement

Palatable
(adj.) 1) agreeable 2) tasty

Rosa's parents finally came to a palatable compromise: she would spend weekends with her mom and weekdays with her dad.

Word family: palate
Synonyms: 1) acceptable 2) appetizing

Pan
(v.) to criticize

The movie was panned by critics

Synonyms: attack, lambaste

Panacea
(n.) a solution that cures all problems

She thought that more money would be the panacea to solve all their problems.

Synonyms: cure-all

Paramount

(adj.) having superior power and influence

The mother's paramount concern was for the health of her child.

Synonyms: important

_____
_____
_____
_____

Parch

(v.) to make very thirsty

The sun parched all the crops growing in the field.

Word family: parched
Synonyms: scorch, roast

_____
_____
_____
_____

Pardon

(v.) to forgive

My coach pardoned me for all the practices I missed.

Synonyms: excuse

_____
_____
_____
_____

Parody

(n.) a humorous imitation

The play was a modern parody of Shakespeare's original work.

Synonyms: satire

_____
_____
_____

Pedantic

(adj.) overly academic, boring

The teacher's lesson was so pedantic that no student could understand it.

Word family: pedant
Synonyms: scrupulous, precise

_____
_____
_____

114

Penitent

(adj.) feeling regret for doing something wrong

I was truly penitent after cheating on the test.

Word family: penance
Synonyms: repentant, contrite

_____

_____

_____

_____

Penurious

(adj). poor

She remembered her penurious childhood, thankful for the way her circumstances had changed.

Synonyms: poverty-stricken

_____

_____

_____

_____

Peripheral

(adj.) 1) on the edge, 2) unimportant

Emily is peripheral to our friend group. She usually hangs out with other people.

Word family: periphery
Synonyms: outer, edge

_____

_____

_____

_____

Permeate

(v.) spread

The idea permeated the classroom.

Synonyms: pervade

_____

_____

_____

Pernicious

(adj.) extremely harmful, deadly, fatal

Lyme disease is a pernicious disease often caused by ticks.

Synonyms: harmful, damaging

_____

_____

_____

Directions:

Fill in the blanks using the words in the box. No word should be used more than once.

If you need help, first write the definition next to the vocab word in the box. Then find the best sentence for the word.

Obstructing	Ominous	Opulent	Orator	Pact
Palatable	Panacea	Pardoned	Peripheral	Pernicious

1. A big tree had fallen in the middle of the road, _____ our route home.

2. At first, I was angry with my friend for betraying me, but after he apologized, I _____ his mistake.

3. I don't think it's fair that some people live _____ lives filled with riches and vacations, and some people don't have enough money to buy food.

4. Jesse is a _____ member of our friend group; sometimes he hangs out with us and sometimes he hangs out with other people.

5. Esmeralda and Emily made a _____ to be best friends forever.

6. The dark storm clouds rolling in were _____.They foreshadowed a coming storm.

7. Money isn't a _____ for all problems. After all, money doesn't buy happiness.

8. Mold is a type of fungus that has a _____ effect. It can harm people's health and make people very sick.

9. I think chocolate is the most _____ food of all. If I could eat chocolate for breakfast and dinner, I would.

10. Cicero was a famous Roman _____, known widely for his public speeches.

Directions:

Select the best synonym for the vocabulary word.

1. Obscure
   a. Abundant
   b. Unknown
   c. Prominent
   d. Incompetent

2. Obsolete
   a. Inevitable
   b. Outdated
   c. Exalted
   d. Useful

3. Obstinate
   a. Irate
   b. Adamant
   c. Peripheral
   d. Indicted

4. Opaque
   a. Nontransparent
   b. Transparent
   c. Ogle
   d. Creative

5. Open-handed
   a. Benevolent
   b. Generous
   c. Languorous
   d. Pleasant

6. Oration
   a. Speech
   b. Lambast
   c. Juxtaposition
   d. Trepidation

7. Ostentatious
   a. Flamboyant
   b. Thrifty
   c. Greedy
   d. Royal

8. Pan
   a. Overdue
   b. Hurry
   c. Criticize
   d. Invalidate

9. Paramount
   a. Important
   b. Lithe
   c. Infamous
   d. Hasty

10. Parch
    a. Endure
    b. Roast
    c. Fathom
    d. Satisfy

11. Parody
    a. Bliss
    b. Imitation
    c. Novice
    d. Facet

12. Pedantic
    a. Sympathetic
    b. Boring
    c. Contrite
    d. Perfect

13. Penitent
    a. Scholarly
    b. Withdrawn
    a. Enigmatic
    b. Contrite

14. Penurious
    a. Malicious
    b. Dull
    c. Poor
    d. Impudent

15. Permeate
    a. Spread
    b. Peripheral
    c. Celebrate
    d. Repent

Find the answer key for all sections on page 171

The Fifteenth Set: Perpetuate—Profanity

Directions: Read the vocab word card. Then write your own sentence using the vocab word.

Perpetuate

(v.) to continue, to preserve

Lydia's bad behavior only served to perpetuate her teacher's negative opinion of her.

Word family: perpetual
Synonyms: maintain, carry on

_____

_____

_____

_____

Peruse

(v.) to read or examine carefully

Caleb perused all the delicious food, deciding what to eat next.

Word family: perusing
Synonyms: scrutinize, examine, investigate

_____

_____

_____

_____

Pilfer

(v.) to steal

Sarai caught her sister pilfering her closet.

Synonyms: plunder, steal, pillage

_____

_____

_____

_____

Pious

(adj.) deeply religious

The pious man prayed every day.

Word family: piety
Synonyms: religious, devout, devoted

_____

_____

_____

_____

Placate

(v.) to quiet down, appease

I tried to placate the crying baby with a lullaby.

Synonyms: appease, pacify, calm

_____

_____

_____

_____

Plaintive
(adj.) sounding sad and mournful

At the animal shelter, the dog's plaintive look was heartbreaking.

Synonyms: mournful, sorrowful, wistful

Plausible
(adj.) possible or believable

Jazmin did not believe in fairytales. She thought they were implausible.

Word family: plausibility
Synonyms: possible, believable, feasible

Plight
(n.) a bad situation

He sighed, knowing that at this moment there wasn't anything to do about his plight but wait.

Synonyms: predicament, trouble, difficulty

Plumage
(n.) the feathers on a bird

The parrot's plumage was especially colorful.

Synonyms: feathers, mantle

Plunder
(v.) to steal

Vikings were known for plundering neighboring villages.

Synonyms: pillage, loot, raid

Polymorphous

(adj.) having many shapes

Families come in all shapes and sizes; they are polymorphous.

Word family: morph, amorphous
Synonyms: multiform, multifarious

_____

Posterity

(n.) future generations

The statue celebrated the heroes for all posterity.

Synonyms: progeny, descendants

_____

Potable

(adj.) suitable for drinking

Some places in the United States do not have potable water because of bad environmental policies.

Word family: pot
Synonyms: drinkable

_____

Potent

(adj.) having great power or being effective

The magic potion was potent. One drop was enough for a powerful spell.

Word family: potential
Synonyms: powerful, strong, effective

_____

Pragmatic

(adj.) practical or useful

I tried to make a pragmatic decision, so I chose to purchase a pair of jeans over a fancy ballroom gown.

Synonyms: practical, sensible, realistic

Preamble
(n.) an introduction to a formal document

The preamble to the constitution sets the stage for the constitution of the United States.

Synonyms: introduction

_____

_____

_____

_____

Precedence
(n.) being more important than something or someone else

His desire for power took precedence over anything else, and he became power-hungry and cruel.

Word family: precedent, precede
Synonyms: priority

_____

_____

_____

_____

Predominantly
(adj.) being larger in number, quantity, power, status

The debate team was predominantly female, but there were a few male team members.

Word family: dominate
Synonyms: prevail

_____

_____

_____

_____

Premise
(n.) a summary or conclusion

The premise of the book was that no two people are the same.

Synonyms: conclusion, hypothesis

_____

_____

_____

_____

Presume
(v.) to assume

Don't presume to know the truth.

Synonyms: assume

_____

_____

_____

_____

Primitive

(adj.) 1) having to do with an early stage of some development 2) simple

Primitive humans learned how to use fire and how to farm to make survival easier.

Synonyms: 1) early, primary 2) plain, basic

Privation

(n). lack of necessities

The privation in the community meant that many families went hungry.

Word family: deprive, deprivation
Synonyms: hardship, destitution, poverty

Procure

(v.) to obtain

She knew she needed to procure medicine if she was going to get healthier.

Word family: procure
Synonyms: achieve, get

Profane

(v/adj.) treating someone/something with disrespect

The conservative church accused the book of being profane because the author wrote that God was a woman.

Word family: profanity
Synonyms: debase, degrade

Profanity

(n.) offensive language

My mom does not allow profanity in her house.

Word family: profane
Synonyms: swear word, obscenity, curse

Directions:

Fill in the blanks using the words in the box. No word should be used more than once.

If you need help, first write the definition next to the vocab word in the box. Then find the best sentence for the word.

Peruse	Pilfering	Placate	Plausible	Plight
Plumage	Potable	Preamble	Premise	Presumed

1. I always like to _____ the candy aisle at the grocery store, deciding which

    ones I like the best and determining which ones I want to buy.

2. A male peacock's _____ is very colorful, filled with blues and greens.

3. The _____ of the book was about a young wizard who saves the world with

    the help of some courage and loyal friends.

4. By the smile on my mom's face, I _____ she was proud of my ballet

    performance.

5. The _____ of the United States Constitution introduces the document and

    presents the principles of the nation.

6. My brother thinks that mermaids are real. I think that is not _____.

7. I caught my brother _____ the kitchen cabinets, looking for cookies

    and snacks.

8. Because water is essential for human life, all humans have the right to

    _____ water.

9. I tried to _____ the crying baby by singing to her and offering her candy.

10. Tom sighed, knowing that at this moment, there wasn't anything to do about his unfortunate

    _____. He would just need to wait until tomorrow.

Directions:

Select the best synonym for the vocabulary word.

1. Perpetuate
   a. Spoil
   b. Maintain
   c. Obdurate
   d. Volatile

2. Pious
   a. Nautical
   b. Religious
   c. Plunder
   d. Nimble

3. Plaintive
   a. Indifferent
   b. Benevolent
   c. Mournful
   d. Impediment

4. Plunder
   a. Alleviate
   b. Integrate
   c. Pillage
   d. Obscure

5. Polymorphous
   a. Tenacious
   b. Amorphous
   c. Notorious
   d. Tedious

6. Posterity
   a. Progeny
   b. Award
   c. Ingenious
   d. Innate

7. Potent
   a. Powerful
   b. Infamous
   c. Adamant
   d. Hidden

8. Pragmatic
   a. Imperious
   b. Regal
   c. Practical
   d. Luminary

9. Precedence
   a. Priority
   b. Splendor
   c. Caution
   d. Competence

10. Predominantly
    a. Prevailing
    b. Shameful
    c. Pristine
    d. Public

11. Primitive
    a. Nomadic
    b. Scowling
    c. Basic
    d. Opaque

12. Privation
    a. Peripheral
    b. Hardship
    c. Hue
    d. Domestic

13. Procure
    a. Delight
    b. Achieve
    c. Obscure
    d. Waver

14. Profane
    a. Exalt
    b. Annoy
    c. Debase
    d. Ebullient

15. Profanity
    a. Obscenity
    b. Rhetoric
    c. Remove
    d. Euphoria

Find the answer key for all sections on page 171

The Sixteenth Set: Prolific—Recuperate

Directions: Read the vocab word card. Then write your own sentence using the vocab word.

Prolific
(adj.) 1) productive 2) plentiful

She was a prolific writer who wrote over 100 hundred children's books across her career.

Synonyms: 1) creative, productive 2) abundant

_____

_____

_____

_____

Propagate
(v.) to reproduce or multiply

The group propagated a lie.

Word family: propagation
Synonyms: grow, breed, spread, increase

_____

_____

_____

Prophetic
(adj.) predicting the future

I had a prophetic dream in which I won the lottery. The next day I actually did win the lottery!

Word family: prophet, prophecy
Synonyms: prescient

_____

_____

_____

Prosperous
(adj.) wealthy or fortunate

The business was very prosperous. Sales grew every year.

Word family: prosper
Synonyms: thriving, successful

_____

_____

_____

Provisional
(adj.) existing in the present, possibly to change in the future

My parents said that my birthday party was provisional on me getting good grades. If I didn't get good grades, we wouldn't have a party!

Word family: provision
Synonyms: temporary, conditional

_____

_____

_____

Prudent

(adj.) careful and well-planned

It would be a prudent decision to start saving money now.

Word family: prudence
Synonyms: wise, careful, shrewd

_____

_____

_____

_____

Pugnacious

(adj.) quick to fight or argue

Because of Courtney's pugnacious behavior, she had very few friends.

Word family: pugnacity
Synonyms: hostile, aggressive, combative, antagonistic

_____

_____

_____

_____

Pungent

(adj.) a strong sharp taste or smell

Garlic is a particularly pungent food. You can smell it from across the room!

Synonyms: strong, aromatic

_____

_____

_____

_____

Purist

(n.) a person who insists on following traditions and rules

My grandmother is a purist when it comes to making Italian food. When we make food with her, we have to follow strict recipes and only use the highest quality ingredients.

Word family: pure, puritan
Synonyms: perfectionist, traditionalist

_____

_____

_____

_____

Quandary

(n.) problem

I didn't know who to sit with in the cafeteria. I solved my quandary by taking my lunch outside.

Synonyms: dilemma, predicament

_____

_____

_____

Quarrelsome
(adj.) argumentative

When I get hungry, I can be really quarrelsome. My mom told me that dinner would be 5 minutes late and I started to argue with her!

Word family: quarrel
Synonyms: bickering, confrontational

_____
_____
_____
_____

Quell
(v.) 1) to calm 2) to stop

Luca tried to calm my fears.

Synonyms: 1) subdue, pacify, 2) end, crush

_____
_____
_____
_____

Quibble
(v.) to complain about little things

My sisters quibble over the smallest things. Yesterday, they fought over a spoon!

Word family: quip
Synonyms: grumble, complain

_____
_____
_____
_____

Quiver
(v.) to tremble

I felt the earth quiver, and I knew we'd just experienced an earthquake.

Word family: quivering
Synonyms: shake, shiver, quaver

_____
_____
_____
_____

Ramble
(v.) to move or speak without direction

When I get excited about a topic, I can just ramble on about it forever.

Word family: rambling
Synonyms: chatter, babble, meander

_____
_____
_____
_____

Rancid

(adj.) having a nasty smell or taste, rotting

I knew the milk had gone bad by its rancid smell.

Synonyms: sour, rotten, stale, putrid

Rancorous

(adj.) showing hatred or ill-will

The conversation became rancorous and eventually the two classmates began to yell loudly at each other.

Word family: rancor
Synonyms: bitter, spiteful, hateful, resentful

Ratify

(v.) to approve, usually a law

Congress needed to ratify the new law by January 1st.

Word family: ratification, ratifying
Synonyms: confirm, endorse, approve

Ravenous

(adj.) extremely hungry

I accidentally skipped lunch and was ravenous by dinner time.

Synonyms: starving, famished

Rebuke

(v.) to criticize sharply

My teacher rebuked the class for having a food fight at lunch.

Synonyms: admonish, scold, castigate

Recalcitrant

(adj.) disobedient

My cat can be very recalcitrant when she wants food.

Word family: recalcitrance
Synonyms: uncooperative, intractable

Recede

(v). to move away or become smaller

Over time, the shoreline began to recede until eventually the lake completely dried up.

Word family: receding, recession
Synonyms: retreat, diminish, decrease

Recluse

(n.) someone who lives a solitary life and tends to avoid others

The man was a recluse who rarely left his home.

Word family: reclusive
Synonyms: hermit

Recreation

(n.) something done for fun like a hobby or game

My favorite recreational activities are playing soccer, singing in choir, and talking to my friends.

Word family: recreational
Synonyms: leisure, fun

Recuperate

(v.) to heal or return to good health

After I broke my ankle, I needed to take some time to recuperate.

Word family: recuperation
Synonyms: recover

Directions:

Fill in the blanks using the words in the box. No word should be used more than once.

If you need help, first write the definition next to the vocab word in the box. Then find the best sentence for the word.

Prolific	Prosperous	Prudent	Pungent	Quandary
Rancorous	Ravenous	Recreation	Recluse	Recuperate

1. My favorite things to do for _____ are soccer and drawing.

2. I forgot my lunch money at home so by the end of the school day I was

   _____ .

3. Saving your money from an early age is a _____ financial decision.

4. I found myself in a _____: should I choose to go out with my friends or

   stay at home to study for my test?

5. I needed physical therapy to _____ my broken arm.

6. The conversation became _____ when the two classmates began

   to yell at each other.

7. He was a _____ artist, who painted hundreds of paintings throughout

   his career.

8. The _____ smell of fried onions filled the kitchen.

9. The successful entrepreneur founded a very _____ business.

10. Harper Lee is a famous author. Most people don't know that she was also a

    _____, who preferred not to leave the comforts of her home.

Directions:

Select the best synonym for the vocabulary word.

1. Propagate
    a. Retreat
    b. Multiply
    c. Subdue
    d. Recover

2. Prophetic
    a. Weak
    b. Ambiguous
    c. Prescient
    d. Joyous

3. Provisional
    a. Pithy
    b. Conditional
    c. Predicated
    d. Wondrous

4. Pugnacious
    a. Willing
    b. Hostile
    c. Fertile
    d. Pleasant

5. Purist
    a. Thriving
    b. Traditionalist
    c. Amorphous
    d. Careful

6. Quarrelsome
    a. Creative
    b. Argumentative
    c. Problematic
    d. Amorphous

7. Quell
    a. Procure
    b. Pacify
    c. Debase
    d. Pillage

8. Quibble
    a. Sabotage
    b. Construe
    c. Complain
    d. Mitigate

9. Quiver
    a. Pan
    b. Withdraw
    c. Tremble
    d. Flex

10. Ramble
    a. Chatter
    b. Audible
    c. Scold
    d. Linger

11. Rancid
    a. Molten
    b. Notorious
    c. Rotting
    d. Palatable

12. Ratify
    a. Protrude
    b. Approve
    c. Rouse
    d. Obstruct

13. Rebuke
    a. Scold
    b. Orate
    c. Resent
    d. Avoid

14. Recalcitrant
    a. Inevitable
    b. Natural
    c. Disobedient
    d. Irate

15. Recede
    a. Insinuate
    b. Diminish
    c. Mock
    d. Bury

Find the answer key for all sections on page 171

The Seventeenth Set: Rehabilitate—Salutation

Directions: Read the vocab word card. Then write your own sentence using the vocab word.

Rehabilitate
(v.) to restore to good condition (usually with
therapy or education)

*It took six months of rehabilitation to six my broken
ankle.*

Word family: rehab, rehabilitation
Synonyms: restore, renew, fix

_____

_____

_____

_____

Relic
(n.) ancient object

Museums are filled with old relics from history.

Synonyms: artifact

_____

_____

_____

_____

Relinquish
(v.) to renounce

*I had to relinquish my favorite t-shirt because I
grew too big for it.*

Synonyms: give up

_____

_____

_____

_____

Reminisce
(v.) to think of the past

*Sometimes I reminisce about how easy elementary
school was.*

Word family: reminiscent
Synonyms: recollect, remember

_____

_____

_____

_____

Remote
(adj.) distant

*Remote learning is challenging because you never
get to see your friends.*

Synonyms: far away, secluded

_____

_____

_____

Renaissance

(n.) a rebirth or revival

The period of the 14th-17h century in Europe is called the Renaissance because there was a renewed interest in art, literature, and philosophy.

Synonyms: resurgence

Rendezvous

(n.) a meeting, usually in secret

They were invited to the midnight rendezvous.

Synonyms: meeting, appointment, tryst

Renege

(v.) to go back on a promise or contract

Even though I initially agreed to go to the mall with my friend, I had so much homework I had to renege on our plans.

Synonyms: retract, go back on

Renounce

(n.) to give up or resign something

My new year's resolution is to renounce my bad habit of chewing my nails.

Synonyms: reject, relinquish

Repent

(v.) to feel sorry and regretful

On the day of the test, he repented his decision not to study.

Word family: repenting
Synonyms: regret, rue

Replete
(adj.) filled with something

The dinner table was replete with delicious-looking food. She couldn't wait to try all the dishes.

Synonyms: abundant, full

_____

Repugnant
(adj.) highly disgusting

I think that spinach is a repugnant vegetable.

Word family: repugnancy, repugnance
Synonyms: offensive

_____

Residual
(adj.) left over, remaining

My mom sent me to the store to buy milk, and I used the residual change to buy myself a candy bar.

Word family: residue
Synonyms: remaining, excess, persisting

_____

Retrospect
(n.) review of past events

In retrospect, I probably shouldn't have eaten so much sugar before bed.

Word family: retrospective
Synonyms: hindsight

_____

Revere
(v.) to deeply respect or admire

I really revere Harriet Tubman for her courage.

Word family: reverence, reverent, reverential
Synonyms: respect, esteem, appreciation

Reverent
(adj.) respectful, worshipful

I am very reverent of Harriet Tubman and her courage.

Word family: reverence, revere, reverential
Synonyms: respectful, worshipping, admiring

_____
_____
_____
_____

Rhetorician
(n.) something larger in number, quantity, power, or status

His desire for power took precedence over anything else, and he became power-hungry and cruel.

Word family: rhetoric
Synonyms: orator

_____
_____
_____
_____

Rift
(n.) 1) a narrow crack in something 2) a break in friendly relations

My friend and I are in a rift because we disagree about who is right and who is wrong.

Synonyms: 1) split, crack 2) quarrel, fight

_____
_____
_____
_____

Rigor
(n.) 1) the quality of being challenging 2) the quality of being inflexible

The teacher was known for the rigor of her classroom and her strict expectations.

Word family: rigorous
Synonyms: 1) challenge 2) strictness, severity

_____
_____
_____
_____

Rigorous
(adj.) 1) challenging 2) inflexible

My school has a very rigorous curriculum. It can be quite challenging.

Word family: rigor
Synonyms: 1) difficult 2) strict, severe

_____
_____
_____
_____

Robust
(adj.) strong and healthy

The coach made sure all the players had a robust exercise routine. They always left practice sweaty and exhausted.

Synonyms: powerful, vigorous

Rout
(n). defeat

The Battle of Quebec was a major military rout for the American military.

Synonyms: retreat, conquer, vanquish

Rue
(v.) to regret

You will rue the day you were mean to me.

Word family: rueful
Synonyms: regret, lament

Ruse
(n.) a clever trick

James created a ruse to keep Clemence away from her house so her friends could decorate it for her surprise party.

Synonyms: ploy, scheme

Salutation
(n.) greeting

In Hawaii, it's common to hear "Aloha" as an everyday salutation.

Word family: salute
Synonyms: welcome, hail, greeting

Directions:

Fill in the blanks using the words in the box. No word should be used more than once.

If you need help, first write the definition next to the vocab word in the box. Then find the best sentence for the word.

Relic	Reminisce	Rendezvous	Remote	Replete
Retrospect	Revere	Rigorous	Rue	Salutation

1. My grandmother likes to _____ about what the world used to be like when she was a child.

2. I _____ my decision to watch TV rather than study for the big English test.

3. Bonjour is a French _____ that translates to hello.

4. The table was set for a big family dinner, _____ with all my favorite foods.

5. In _____, it was probably a bad idea to watch TV rather than study for the big English test.

6. _____ learning can be difficult because you have to be independent and you don't get a lot of help from your teacher.

7. I _____ my grandfather, who is the hardest working person I know.

8. The math curriculum at my new school is very _____. Sometimes it's so challenging that I need tutoring from my teacher.

9. Romeo and Juliet were forbidden from seeing each other. However, they met for a secret _____.

10. Museums are filled with _____ from history.

Directions:

Select the best synonym for the vocabulary word.

1. Rehabilitate
   a. Portray
   b. Restore
   c. Mar
   d. Laud

2. Relinquish
   a. Complicate
   b. Refute
   c. Renounce
   d. Innovate

3. Renaissance
   a. Prophecy
   b. Elegance
   c. Revival
   d. Satire

4. Renege
   a. Vary
   b. Retract
   c. Illuminate
   d. Founder

5. Renounce
   a. Relinquish
   b. Exile
   c. Exclude
   d. Portray

6. Repent
   a. Apologize
   b. Sincere
   c. Dilute
   d. Invalidate

7. Repugnant
   a. Emanating
   b. Disgusting
   c. Demure
   d. Abandoned

8. Residual
   a. Remaining
   b. Deft
   c. Conventional
   d. Scarcity

9. Reverent
   a. Opulent
   b. Abundant
   c. Worshipful
   d. Passive

10. Rhetorician
    a. Orator
    b. Glutton
    c. Politician
    d. Incumbent

11. Rift
    a. Crack
    b. Burden
    c. Jest
    d. Simulation

12. Rigor
    a. Null
    b. Challenge
    c. Polite
    d. Boring

13. Robust
    a. Prominent
    b. Merry
    c. Strong
    d. Obscure

14. Rout
    a. Vanquish
    b. Ignore
    c. Forewarn
    d. Impede

15. Ruse
    a. Barricade
    b. Ploy
    c. Periphery
    d. Agreement

Find the answer key for all sections on page 171

The Eighteenth Set: Salve—Stark

Directions: Read the vocab word card. Then write your own sentence using the vocab word.

Salve
(n.) something used to heal or soothe

My mom told me to apply a salve on my poison ivy rash.

Synonyms: ointment, treatment, cure

_____

_____

_____

Sanctimonious
(adj.) acting morally superior, holier-than-thou

My sister acts sanctimonious when she thinks I did something wrong.

Word family: sanctity, sanctimony
Synonyms: pious, self-righteous

_____

_____

_____

Sarcastic
(adj.) using witty language used to insult or show displeasure

I was hurt by my brother's sarcastic joke.

Word family: sarcasm
Synonyms: sardonic, ironic, satirical

_____

_____

_____

Satire
(n.) the use of humor, irony, or exaggeration

In satire, it is very common to have characters make fun of real people and events.

Word family: satirical
Synonyms: sarcasm, mockery, parody

_____

_____

_____

Scold
(v.) to criticize

My teacher scolded the class for having a food fight at lunch.

Word family: scolding
Synonyms: reprimand, admonish, rebuke

_____

_____

_____

Scorn
(n.) lack of respect and a strong feeling of dislike

Jacques felt scorn for the person who lied to him.

Word family: scornful
Synonyms: contempt, dislike

Scornful
(adj.) a strong feeling of dislike

Jacques felt scornful about the person who lied to him.

Word family: scorn
Synonyms: contemptuous

Scourge
(n.) someone or something that causes others trouble or suffering

Lice and bedbugs are two types of bugs that are a scourge to cities. They can spread quickly amongst large groups of people.

Synonyms: affliction, problem, curse

Scruples
(n.) feelings of doubt or guilt about a suggested action

She had scruples about skipping class.

Word family: scrupulous, unscrupulous
Synonyms: hesitation, reservation, reluctance

Scrutinize
(v.) to examine closely

My teacher scrutinized my homework, looking for errors.

Word family: scrutiny
Synonyms: peruse, inspect, study

Sedate

(v.) to calm, especially by use of drug

I took a sleeping pill to help sedate myself.

Word family: sedative
Synonyms: tranquilize, calm

_____

_____

_____

_____

Shrewd

(adj.) very clever and smart, tricky

I tried to be shrewd with my money, saving as much as I could.

Word family: shrewdly
Synonyms: astute, sharp-witted, intelligent

_____

_____

_____

Slander

(n.) a false and mean-spirited statement meant to harm someone's reputation

One example of slander that I have experienced is this: one time, someone tried to spread a nasty rumor about me at school.

Word family: slanderous
Synonyms: defamation, lie, untruth, insult

_____

_____

_____

_____

Solemn

(adj.) not cheerful or smiling; very serious

The day my parents told me we were moving away from our friends and family was a very solemn day.

Word family: solemnity
Synonyms: serious, sober, somber, dignified

_____

_____

_____

_____

Solidify

(v.) strengthen

My teacher told me I needed to solidify my essay with more evidence from the text.

Word family: solid, solidification
Synonyms: reinforce, bolster

_____

_____

_____

Somber

(adj.) serious, dark, or gloomy

There was a somber mood when my parents told me our family was moving away from all our family and friends.

Synonyms: dark, dull, gloomy, solemn

Sporadic

(adj.) having no pattern or order

Snow days happen sporadically throughout the winter.

Word family: sporadically
Synonyms: irregular, random, infrequent

Sprawl

(v.) to sit, lie, or fall with one's arms and legs spread out

The man was sprawled out on the subway, taking up three seats.

Word family: sprawling
Synonyms: lounge, lie

Spur

(v.) to encourage or incentivize someone or some action

Even though she was tired, her pride spurred her to keep practicing. She didn't want to lose.

Synonyms: stimulate, encourage, support

Spurious

(adj.) fake or false

Carl was fired from his job for making a spurious claim.

Synonyms: invalid, illegitimate, fictitious

Squalid

(adj.) extremely dirty and unpleasant

The apartment was squalid. It looked like it hadn't been cleaned in years.

Word family: squalor
Synonyms: filthy, grimy, improper

Squander

(v). to waste something

Don't ever squander an opportunity to learn a new skill.

Word family: squandering
Synonyms: waste, throw away, misuse

Stagnate

(v.) to become inactive or dull

Over time the rushing river began to stagnate until the water no longer moved, and it became a large lake.

Word family: stagnation
Synonyms: stand, do nothing, not move

Staid

(adj.) straitlaced and serious

My staid grandmother always wants me to act prim and proper.

Synonyms: quiet, steady, rule-following, boring

Stark

(adj.) bare, without decoration

My grandfather's house is starkly decorated, with no decorations and very little furniture.

Word family: starkly
Synonyms: somber, gloomy, undecorated, uninviting

Directions:

Fill in the blanks using the words in the box. No word should be used more than once.

If you need help, first write the definition next to the vocab word in the box. Then find the best sentence for the word.

Scolded	Scrutinized	Sedate	Solemn	Sporadically
Sprawled	Spurred	Squander	Stagnate	Stark

1. My father _____ me for waking up late and missing the school bus.

2. By the _____ look on everyone's faces, I knew something bad had happened.

3. My basketball coach tells me not to _____ my talent. She says I'm very talented, but I need to practice if I'm going to play on a good college team.

4. In California, it rains _____. One month it won't rain at all; other months it will for a week straight.

5. Certain vitamins and supplements can _____ you. For example, some people take melatonin, a supplement to help them calm down and fall asleep.

6. My teacher _____ my essay, looking to make sure my argument and evidence were clear.

7. My classroom is very _____, with very little color or art on the walls.

8. Even though I was tired, my pride _____ me to keep practicing. I knew that if I kept practicing, I could win Saturday's competition.

9. My room was so messy that you couldn't see the floor because all my toys were _____ around the room.

10. Over time, the rushing water began to _____ until one day, the water no longer moved. Two years later, the water had all dried up and the river had disappeared.

Directions:
Select the best synonym for the vocabulary word.

1. Salve
   a. Frock
   b. Ointment
   c. Jeer
   d. Frown

2. Sanctimonious
   a. Self-righteous
   b. Questioning
   c. Impervious
   d. Accusing

3. Sarcastic
   a. Ironic
   b. Opulent
   c. Invalid
   d. Sorrowful

4. Satire
   a. Verbal
   b. Sarcasm
   c. Lambaste
   d. Precision

5. Scorn
   a. Fury
   b. Contempt
   c. Irreverent
   d. Novel

6. Scornful
   a. Regretful
   b. Contemptuous
   c. Joyful
   d. Poisonous

7. Scourge
   a. Affliction
   b. Hesitation
   c. Inactivity
   d. Partisan

8. Scruples
   a. Seriousness
   b. Reservations
   c. Periodic
   d. Immoral

9. Shrewd
   a. Lavish
   b. Loving
   c. Astute
   d. Special

10. Slander
    a. Uplift
    b. Lie
    c. Defeat
    d. Excuse

11. Solidify
    a. Permeate
    b. Strengthen
    c. Forgive
    d. Humor

12. Somber
    a. Gloomy
    b. Polite
    c. Violation
    d. Peripheral

13. Spurious
    a. Superstitious
    b. Fictitious
    c. Ruse
    d. Perfect

14. Squalid
    a. Dirty
    b. Forthright
    c. Meticulous
    d. Clever

15. Staid
    a. Pallid
    b. Imperfect
    c. Serious
    d. Uproot

Find the answer key for all sections on page 171

The Nineteenth Set: Steadfast—Transpose

Directions: Read the vocab word card. Then write your own sentence using the vocab word.

Steadfast
(adj.) loyal and constant

Anna is my most steadfast friend. She is always there for me.

Word family: steadfastly
Synonyms: committed, faithful, devoted, unwavering, unswerving

_____

_____

_____

_____

Stifle
(v.) to hold back or smother

Some students think that school uniforms stifle their creativity.

Word family: stifling
Synonyms: suffocating, smothering, suppressing, restraining

_____

_____

_____

_____

Subjective
(adj.) influenced by personal opinion

There is no right answer to the question, "Who is the best musician ever?" It is a subjective question.

Synonyms: biased, partisan

_____

_____

_____

_____

Sublime
(adj.) very beautiful or perfect

I think that chocolate cake is sublime!

Synonyms: awesome, wonderful

_____

_____

_____

_____

Succinct
(v.) briefly and clearly expressed

It's important to write succinctly. No one wants to read a 20-page essay.

Word family: succinctly
Synonyms: concise, short, brief

_____

_____

_____

_____

Superficial

(adj.) 1) on or near the surface, 2) fake

Sometimes my friends can act really superficial.

Synonyms: 1) shallow 2) false, inauthentic

_____

Superfluous

(adj.) more than what is required or needed

We decided to donate our superfluous food to the food shelter.

Synonyms: unnecessary, extra, redundant

_____

Surmise

(v.) to believe that something is true without having evidence to confirm it

Based on the loud music next door, I could surmise that my neighbors were having a party.

Word family: surmising
Synonyms: guess, conjecture, suspect

_____

Surrogate

(n.) a substitute

My aunt acted as a surrogate mother while my mom was away on business.

Synonyms: replacement, proxy

_____

Sustain

(v.) to support

You need to eat and drink enough every day to be able to sustain your energy.

Word family: sustainability, sustainable
Synonyms: assist, help, encourage

Taxing

(adj.) requiring a lot of effort (either physically or mentally)

Rock climbing is a very taxing activity.

Word family: tax
Synonyms: exhausting, demanding

_____

_____

_____

_____

Temperament

(n.) your usual mood or behavior

My father has a very outgoing temperament and is always the most social person in the room.

Word family: temperamental
Synonyms: personality, disposition

_____

_____

_____

_____

Tenacious

(adj.) holding on to something strongly and persistently

It's important to pursue your dreams tenaciously, even in the face of challenges.

Word family: tenacity
Synonyms: persistent, determined

_____

_____

_____

_____

Tepid

(adj.) neither hot nor cold

By the time I got out of my long bath, the water had turned tepid.

Synonyms: lukewarm, unenthusiastic

_____

_____

_____

_____

Thesis

(n.) a statement that summarizes the claim of an argument

Every essay should include a strong thesis.

Synonyms: theory, claim, argument

_____

_____

_____

_____

Thorough

(adj.) done with great care and completeness

I always make sure to thoroughly plan my essays before I write.

Word family: thoroughly
Synonyms: meticulous, scrupulous

_____

_____

_____

_____

Thrifty

(adj.) able to handle money wisely, not extravagant

It's important to be thrifty when you're trying to save money.

Word family: thrift, spendthrift
Synonyms: prudent, economical, frugal

_____

_____

_____

Timid

(adj.) showing a lack of courage or confidence

I can be very timid in new social situations.

Word family: timidly
Synonyms: reserved, shy, meek, bashful

_____

_____

_____

_____

Toil

(v.) to work hard

My grandparent was a farmer who toiled out in the fields during each harvest.

Word family: toiling
Synonyms: labor

_____

_____

_____

Tome

(n.) a book, especially a long and scholarly one

One of the longest tomes ever written is by Marcel Proust.

Synonyms: opus, book, publication, novel

_____

_____

_____

_____

Transgress

(v.) to go beyond a limit or boundary; to disobey

You can be fined for transgressing the parking laws in the city.

Word family: transgression
Synonyms: misbehave, act out, disobey

Transgression

(n). a violation of a law, command, or duty

I regret my past transgressions.

Word family: transgress
Synonyms: offense, crime, wrongdoing

Transient

(adj.) temporary

My uncle is transient, moving from place to place every time he finds a new job.

Word family: transitory, transition
Synonyms: impermanent, fleeting

Translucent

(adj.) almost transparent, able to be seen through clearly

The white curtain was translucent so you could see what was happening outside the window.

Synonyms: colorless, clear see-through, transparent

Transpose

(v.) transfer something to a different place or context

You can transpose the letters of the word "But" to make the word "Tub."

Synonyms: exchange, switch, relocate, interchange

Directions:

Fill in the blanks using the words in the box. No word should be used more than once.

If you need help, first write the definition next to the vocab word in the box. Then find the best sentence for the word.

Stifle	Sublime	Succinctly	Surmised	Temperament
Tepid	Thoroughly	Timid	Transgressions	Transient

1. The chocolate cake was so _____ that I had three pieces!

2. From the frown on my mom's face, I _____ that she was angry.

3. I filled the bathtub with water, and then forgot about it. By the time I got into the bathtub, the water was _____.

4. My brother is very _____ in front of new people. He doesn't talk a lot and prefers to listen to conversations, rather than joining in.

5. My teacher says that it is important to write _____. If you write too many words, readers can get bored or lose interest.

6. My dog has a really pleasant _____. She's always happy to see me and she never bites.

7. Once a month I _____ clean my room. I put away all my clothes and toys, vacuum the floor, and dust the shelves.

8. Musicians live very _____ lifestyles. They have to perform all over the world, so they're constantly moving from city to city.

9. When my friend and I joke in class, we have to _____ our laughter. If the teacher hears us laughing when we're supposed to be reading, he might give us detention.

10. I regret my past _____.

Directions:

Select the best synonym for the vocabulary word.

1. Steadfast
    a. Irregular
    b. Loyal
    c. Defamation
    d. Tranquilize

2. Subjective
    a. Biased
    b. Objective
    c. Wonderful
    d. Meticulous

3. Superficial
    a. Constant
    b. Fake
    c. Authentic
    d. Adept

4. Superfluous
    a. Unnecessary
    b. Skeptical
    c. Unwilling
    d. Concise

5. Surrogate
    a. Omit
    b. Substitute
    c. Prosper
    d. Adhere

6. Sustain
    a. Mar
    b. Force
    c. Support
    d. Distribute

7. Taxing
    a. Toilsome
    b. Boundless
    c. Marginal
    d. Flexible

8. Tenacious
    a. Frivolous
    b. Determined
    c. Incisive
    d. Genuine

9. Thesis
    a. Tome
    b. Portrayal
    c. Claim
    d. Composure

10. Thrifty
    a. Economical
    b. Extravagant
    c. Careless
    d. Trivial

11. Toil
    a. Strengthen
    b. Labor
    c. Resemble
    d. Deteriorate

12. Tome
    a. Progression
    b. Mute
    c. Book
    d. Scarcity

13. Transgress
    a. Repent
    b. Disobey
    c. Lament
    d. Conquer

14. Translucent
    a. Clear
    b. Opaque
    c. Healthy
    d. Nostalgic

15. Transpose
    a. Renounce
    b. Recollect
    c. Tact
    d. Transfer

Find the answer key for all sections on page 171

The Twentieth Set: Trivial—Zenith

Directions: Read the vocab word card. Then write your own sentence using the vocab word.

Trivial
(adj.) unimportant

I shouldn't be upset about something so trivial, but I was very angry that my brother stole my shoes.

Word family: triviality
Synonyms: insignificant, minor

_____

_____

_____

_____

Trumpet
(v.) to announce or declare something for all to hear

The principal trumpeted the success of the school's football team.

Synonyms: proclaim, broadcast

_____

_____

_____

_____

Tryst
(n.) a secret meeting

They agreed to a tryst in the garden at midnight.

Synonyms: rendezvous

_____

_____

_____

_____

Unscrupulous
(adj.) having or showing no moral principles; not honest or fair; dishonest

He was disliked for his unscrupulous behavior.

Word family: scrupulous, scruples
Synonyms: corrupt, immoral, dishonest

_____

_____

_____

_____

Vacuous
(adj.) empty

People mistakenly thought she was vacuous and ditzy just because she had blonde hair.

Synonyms: blank, vacant, dumb

_____

_____

_____

Variegated

(adj.) having many parts or colors

The variegated outfit caught everyone's attention.

Word family: variegate
Synonyms: multicolored, varicolored

Vend

(v.) to sell

I went to the market to vend my fruits and vegetables.

Word family: vendor, vending
Synonyms: sell

Venerate

(v.) to regard with deep respect

Abraham Lincoln is a widely venerated president.

Word family: veneration
Synonyms: revere, respect

Veneration

(n.) great respect

Statues have been built in veneration of Abraham Lincoln.

Word family: venerate
Synonyms: reverence, respect, admiration

Verbatim

(adv.) using exactly the same words

Plagiarizing is when you copy another person's work verbatim.

Synonyms: word for word

Versatile

(adj.) able to do many things well

I am a versatile basketball player. I'm good at defending, shooting, and assisting.

Word family: versatility
Synonyms: adaptable, flexible

_____

_____

_____

_____

Vexation

(n.) discomfort or distress

I often cry when I am overcome by vexation.

Word family: vex
Synonyms: annoyance, irritation, irritability

_____

_____

_____

Vicarious

(adj.) experienced in the imagination through feelings and actions of another person

I live vicariously through the characters of books and movies.

Word family: vicariously
Synonyms: indirect, secondhand

_____

_____

_____

Vigor

(v.) strength and energy

Even though he was an older man, he walked with vigor every day.

Word family: vigorously
Synonyms: robustness, stamina

_____

_____

_____

Virtuoso

(n.) a person with great skill, especially a musician

Beethoven is a very famous virtuoso.

Synonyms: maestro, genius, expert

_____

_____

_____

_____

Vital

(adj.) necessary or essential

Water and air are vital for humans.

Word family: vitality
Synonyms: essential, indispensable, crucial

_____

_____

_____

_____

Vivid

(adj.) very distinct or realistic

I had a vivid dream about eating ice cream in the park.

Word family: vividly
Synonyms: realistic, evocative, bright, colorful

_____

_____

_____

_____

Volatile

(adj.) explosive and unstable

Because their neighbor's mood was volatile, they always made sure never to throw a ball over the fence.

Word family: volatility
Synonyms: explosive, turbulent

_____

_____

_____

_____

Voracious

(adj.) having a huge appetite, greedy, ravenous; excessively eager

I am a voracious reader. I read two books a week on average.

Word family: voracity
Synonyms: insatiable, unquenchable, unappeasable

_____

_____

_____

_____

Waft

(v.) to float gently in the air, to drift

I woke to the smell of bacon wafting into the room.

Word family: wafting
Synonyms: floating, drifting, gliding

_____

_____

_____

_____

Wane

(v.) 1) to decrease gradually 2) weakening in power, size, or importance

As the sun began to wane, the temperature became cooler.

Word family: waning
Synonyms: disappear, decrease, diminish, dwindle, shrink

Whimsical

(adj). determined by chance or fancy instead of reason

I made a whimsical decision to buy an expensive pair of shoes. Later, I regretted this decision.

Word family: whimsy
Synonyms: fanciful, playful, impulsive, capricious

Wily

(adj.) cunning and crafty

The car salesman was a wily talker. He could trick anyone into buying a car they didn't want.

Synonyms: shrewd, clever, astute, sharp, smart

Writhe

(v.) to twist

When I broke my ankle, I was writhing in pain.

Synonyms: squirm, wriggle

Zenith

(n.) the highest point

When the sun is at its zenith, the daily temperature is usually at its hottest.

Synonyms: apex, acme

Directions:

Fill in the blanks using the words in the box. No word should be used more than once.

If you need help, first write the definition next to the vocab word in the box. Then find the best sentence for the word.

Trivial	Trumpeted	Vend	Versatile	Vexation
Virtuoso	Wafted	Wane	Whimsical	Zenith

1. The daily temperature is usually at its hottest when the sun is at its _____.

2. The daily temperature usually decreases when the sun begins to _____.

3. I know I shouldn't be upset over something so _____, but I got really mad at my sister for taking my clothes.

4. Mozart was a very famous _____, who was known for his musical compositions.

5. My decision to join an art club was _____. I've never done art and don't want to be an artist, but I just wanted to try it out.

6. The smell of breakfast _____ from the kitchen and made me hungry.

7. I am a _____ soccer player. I'm fast, good at defending, and good at passing the ball.

8. I could tell that my parents were overcome with _____ when they began to yell at me for forgetting to clean my room.

9. Over the loudspeaker, our principal _____ a new school rule: We would need to wear uniforms every day.

10. I decided to _____ my cookies and cupcakes at the school bake sale.

Directions:

Select the best synonym for the vocabulary word.

1. Tryst
   a. Toil
   b. Rendezvous
   c. Mirth
   d. Tepid

2. Unscrupulous
   a. Corrupt
   b. Moral
   c. Vacant
   d. Encouraging

3. Vacuous
   a. Empty
   b. Somber
   c. Willful
   d. Clever

4. Variegated
   a. Afflicted
   b. Various
   c. Multicolored
   d. Depicted

5. Venerate
   a. Stoic
   b. Revere
   c. Invalidate
   d. Reject

6. Veneration
   a. Sympathetic
   b. Respect
   c. Apologetic
   d. Scornful

7. Verbatim
   a. Celebratory
   b. Identical
   c. Multitude
   d. Laudatory

8. Vex
   a. Seclude
   b. Annoy
   c. Rue
   d. Power

9. Vigor
   a. Composed
   b. Robust
   c. Healing
   d. Secretive

10. Vital
    a. Timid
    b. Astute
    c. Essential
    d. Sharp

11. Vivid
    a. Explosive
    b. Colorful
    c. Quaint
    d. Imperious

12. Volatile
    a. Explosive
    b. Assumptive
    c. Difficult
    d. Profane

13. Voracious
    a. Practical
    b. Insatiable
    c. Descendant
    d. Shrewd

14. Wily
    a. Cunning
    b. Apex
    c. Obscene
    d. Willful

15. Writhe
    a. Limp
    b. Twist
    c. Degrade
    d. Leach

Find the answer key for all sections on page 171

Glossary

Word	Definition	Synonyms
Abdicate	to give up power	to resign, to quit
Abhor	to hate or detest	detest, contempt, somber
Abhorrent	horrible, worthy of being hated	loathsome, abominable
Abominable	horrible or unpleasant	loathsome, detestable, hateful
Abridge	to shorten in length or duration	shorten
Absolve	to free from guilt or blame	liberate, forgive
Abstinence	act or practice of refraining from indulging	self-restraint
Abundant	plentiful	bounty, abundance
Abyss	a bottomless pit	pit, chasm
Academic	having to do with school or education	scholastic, educational, scholarly
Acclimate	to adapt to a new climate, environment, or situation	adapt, adjust
Accord	agreement	agreement, pact, treaty
Accrue	to grow or gather over time	grow, accumulate
Adage	an old saying usually considered to be true	saying, proverb
Adamant	stubborn and persistent	obdurate, adamant, obstinate
Adept	skillful	expert, talented, gifted
Adhere	to stick to	sticky
Adhesion	something that is sticky or used to hold things together	glue
Adjunct	added on; additional	additional, extra
Admiring	regarding with approval or respect	applauding, praising,
Admonish	to warn or reprimand someone firmly	scold
Adverse	unfavorable, challenging	dangerous, challenging
Aggravate	to make worse	annoy
Agitate	to disturb or upset	disturb
Ail	to suffer from sickness or pain	trouble, pain
Akin	related to or alike	related; alike
Allege	to declare, usually without proof	to claim; to assert
Aloof	keeping a distance	distant, withdrawn
Altruistic	doing good for others	generous, philanthropic
Amass	to gather together or accumulate	accumulate, grow
Ambiguous	vague or unclear	vague, debatable
Ambivalent	having opposite or mixed feelings (such as love and hate)	indecisive, uncertain
Ameliorate	to make better; to improve	improve, better
Amiable	friendly, good-natured	pleasant, genial, congenial
Amorphous	without shape	shapeless
Analytical	intending to understand something	critical, scholarly
Anguish	suffering or pain	despair, sorrow
Animosity	hostility	hostility, malevolence, resentment
Antagonize	to annoy or provoke	aggravate
Antics	foolery; unpredictable behavior	pranks, escapades
Apathetic	lack of feeling or interest	indifferent, unconcerned
Appall	to be horrified	horrify, shock
Aptitude	ability	capability, talent
Archaic	very old	ancient
Arduous	hard to do, requiring much effort	strenuous, taxing, difficult
Arid	very dry	dry
Aristocratic	of noble birth; snobbish	noble, elite
Articulate	clearly express	eloquent, communicative
Artifice	deception; trickery	trick, deceit
Ascent	a movement upward; a climb	climb, rise
Aspirant	someone who wants to achieve great things	dreamer, candidate
Assailable	vulnerable	defenseless, weak
Assert	to state a point of view	declare, contend, claim
Assess	to evaluate or determine the worth of something	evaluate, test, judge
Assiduously	hardworking	diligently, laboriously
Astute	smart or clever	quick-witted, sharp
Attain	to achieve	achieve, accomplish

Audible	able to be heard	loud, clear
Augment	to make larger	increase, supplement
Authentic	genuine and true	real, true, genuine
Authoritative	having authority	commanding, strong
Baleful	harmful; menacing	menacing, wicked
Banal	unoriginal and boring	boring
Barbed	spiked	spiky, spiked
Barrage	an overwhelming event or thing happening	bombardment, flood
Bashful	shy	timid, shy
Bedevil	to cause someone a lot of trouble	harass, torment
Begrudge	being reluctant or resentful	resent
Belie	to give a false idea	contradict
Belligerent	hostile and aggressive	hostile, aggressive, combative, antagonistic
Beneficial	resulting in something good	helpful, useful, advantageous
Benevolence	goodness	goodness, kindness, compassion
Benign	harmless	gentle, safe
Berate	to scold sharply	admonish, rebuke, reprimand
Bewilder	to confuse	perplex, befuddle
Bias	favoring one side or opinion over another	partisan, prejudiced
Blight	a disease or problem	disease, affliction
Bolster	to strengthen	support, reinforce
Brackish	having a salty taste and unpleasant to drink	briny
Brash	bold in a rude or pushy way	rude, bold
Brig	the prison of a ship	jail, prison
Briny	salty	brackish
Browbeat	to intimidate	bully
Burgeoning	growing	increasing, developing
Burly	very stocky and muscled	well-built, sturdy
Cacophony	jarring and unpleasant sounds	noise, racket
Calamity	disaster	tragedy
Candid	honest	truthful
Candor	honesty	truth
Capricious	unpredictable and impulsive	fickle, inconstant, mercurial, impulsive
Cast away	1) to throw away 2) to be abandoned after a shipwreck	1) throw away, 2) shipwrecked
Castigate	to scold someone severely	reprimand, admonish, rebuke
Cautious	careful	watchful, wary
Chagrin	embarrassment, disappointment	distress, embarrassment, humiliation
Chasm	1) a deep opening in the earth's surface 2) a large difference between two things	gulf, rift, schism
Choleric	bad-tempered	irritable, grumpy
Chronicle	record in chronological order	account, record
Circulate	1) to move around freely, 2) to spread widely	flow, spread
Circumspect	unwilling to take risks	careful, cautious, wary, prudent
Clandestine	secretive	secret, covert
Clarity	the quality of being easy to see or understand	transparent, clear
Coalesce	to come together	unite, merge
Coerce	to force	compel, persuade
Cognizant	having knowledge or being aware	aware, conscious
Cognize	to perceive, to know, to understand	know, understand, think
Commencement	the beginning of something	beginning
Communal	shared	shared
Competent	good enough	capable, adequate
Complacency	the feeling of being satisfied with how things are and not wanting to change them	self-satisfaction, laziness
Composure	calmness	self-control
Comprehensive	including all or everything	all-inclusive, exhaustive
Concede	to give in or surrender	give up
Condescend	to act as if you are better than someone	patronize
Condone	to forgive or disregard an offense	accept, excuse
Confinement	being restricted or kept in a certain place	imprisonment, enclosed, restricted

Conform	to mold to meet some expectation	obey
Confound	to puzzle or confuse	muddle, bewilder
Congeal	to thicken, or change from liquid to solid	solidify, coagulate
Congenial	agreeable	genial, pleasant
Conscientious	characterized by extreme care and great effort	diligent, industrious
Consensus	an agreement	accord, pact
Console	comfort	comfort, support
Construe	to interpret	interpret, understand
Contempt	extreme dislike or disdain	scorn, dislike
Contemptuous	expressing disdain or extreme dislike	disdainful, scornful
Contentious	inclined to fight or argue	debatable, controversial
Contiguous	lying side by side	adjacent, adjoining, bordering
Contradict	to disagree	deny, challenge, oppose
Contrite	feeling regret for bad behavior	remorseful, regretful, sorry
Contrition	deep regret for doing something wrong	remorse, regret, sorrow
Conventional	traditionally, ordinary	typical, normal
Cordially	politely	polite, pleasant, friendly
Corpulent	overweight	fat
Correlation	A connection between facts or events	connection, association
Counsel	to give advice	advice, guidance
Crevice	a narrow crack, especially in a rock	crack
Cumulative	increasing through successive addition	increasing, growing
Debilitating	weakening, harmful	weakening
Debunk	to prove false	expose, discredit
Decompose	to rot or decay; to break down	decay, break down
Decree	an order or a command	order, edict, command
Deduce	to draw a conclusion from facts	infer
Defer	to delay	detain
Deferment	the act of delaying	detention
Deficient	lacking	lacking, insufficient
Deft	skillful	adept, skillful
Deleterious	harmful	dangerous, detrimental
Delusion	a false opinion or idea	deception
Demure	reserved	shy, meek
Deplorable	horrible	abhorrent
Derelict	abandoned, ruined	run down, neglected
Despair	a feeling of absolute hopelessness	hopelessness, distress
Detain	to stop or hold back	delay, refrain
Detention	the act of keeping back or detaining	confinement
Deteriorate	to worsen	decline
Detractor	a critic	critic
Dexterity	skill or quickness	agility, skill
Dignity	the quality of being worthy of esteem or respect	honor, integrity, respectability
Dilute	to weaken the strength of something, especially by adding water to a solution	weaken, water down
Dingy	dirty, dull, or shabby	gloomy, dark, dismal
Discern	to see clearly, to recognize	insightful, knowledgeable, astute
Discredit	to reject as false	disprove, invalidate
Disingenuous	insincere	fake
Disparage	to criticize or speak badly of	belittle
Disposition	personality	nature, temperament
Dispute	argument	debate
Distort	to bend or twist something out of its normal shape	twist, bend, change
Dormant	temporarily inactive, asleep	resting
Dread	overwhelming fear or to be very afraid	fear
Dubious	doubtful	uncertain, suspicious
Dynamic	energetic, full of movement	energetic, always changing, exciting
Egoist	a self-centered or conceited person	narcissist, self-centered
Egress	to exit	exit
Elaborate	1) very detailed or 2) to provide a detailed explanation	1) detailed, complex 2) explain
Elicit	to draw/bring forth	evoke

Elongate	to lengthen	lengthen, extend
Emanate	1) to spread 2) to originate	emit, exude
Embargo	a ban, especially on trade	ban, restraint, barrier, stoppage
Embroider	1) to sew a design on a piece of cloth 2) to make something more interesting by adding details that are untrue	elaborate, embellish
Embryonic	undeveloped	rudimentary, beginning, initial
Empathetic	having the ability to understand and share the feelings of others	caring, understanding, sensitivity
Emulate	to copy or imitate	imitate, mirror
Enigma	mystery	mystery, puzzle
Ensue	to happen as a result	result, follow, arise
Entrepreneur	creative businessman	businessperson
Epitomize	to be a perfect example	exemplify, embody
Epoch	a large period of time	era
Equate	to equal	correspond, connect, balance
Equivalent	equal	identical
Era	a period of time (usually in the past)	epoch, period
Eradicate	to completely wipe out or destroy	eliminate
Erode	to wear away	fade away
Erudite	having or showing a lot of knowledge	intellectual, knowledgeable, scholarly
Euphony	pleasant, harmonious sound	melody
Euphoria	a feeling of great happiness or well-being	bliss
Evacuate	to leave or withdraw, as from a dangerous situation	remove
Evanescent	lasting a short time, fading away gradually	fleeting, fading
Evoke	to bring up	elicit, stir
Exacerbate	to make worse	aggravate
Exasperate	to make very angry or impatient	infuriate, annoy
Excavate	to dig up	dig
Exclusion	not being allowed to enter or join	banishment; ban, bar
Exile	to banish someone from their native country	banish
Exquisite	beautifully made or designed	beautiful, elegant
Extinct	no longer existing	vanished, dead
Extol	to praise	exalt
Exuberant	overflowing with joy or happiness	ebullient, cheerful
Fabricate	1) to lie; to make up, to invent 2) to manufacturer	make up, fake
Facet	an aspect of something	aspect, feature, dimension
Fallacy	a false or mistaken idea	misconception, misbelief, falsehood
Fathom	to understand	comprehend
Feasible	possible, able to be done	possible, practical, believable, do-able
Felicity	joy and happiness	bliss, delight
Feral	wild and untamed	undomesticated
Fission	a splitting apart	division, splitting
Flamboyant	over the top	ostentatious
Fluctuate	to shift back and forth without regularity	vary, differ, waver
Foment	try to stir up public opinion	incite
Founder	1) to sink; 2) someone who starts a company	1) sink or 2) entrepreneur
Frank	honest and open	candid
Fringe	the edge or outer portion	peripheral
Frugal	not wasteful or extravagant	thrifty
Fundamental	essential	basic
Fusion	a joining together	blend, merging
Garrulous	talkative	loquacious
Gaunt	very thin or bony	skinny, bony, haggard
Genre	a specific style of art or literature	type, kind
Gingerly	carefully	cautiously, with care
Glutton	one who eats and drinks too much, greedy	greedy, insatiable,
Grandeur	grand elegance	splendor
Gregarious	outgoing and social	sociable
Grimace	a facial expression of fear or disapproval	frown, wince, scowl
Grovel	to beg	beg
Hackneyed	overused and old-fashioned	overdone, worn out
Hasty	rushed, sloppy, very quick	hurried
Hilarity	amusement	mirth, merriment

Hoary	1) very old, or 2) gray from old age	hackneyed, banal, old
Hovel	a small, unpleasant building or room	shack
Hue	the color or shade of an object	shade
Idiosyncrasy	a characteristic peculiar to an individual	quirk, peculiarity
Ignoble	dishonorable, shameful	shameful, contemptible
Illuminate	to light up or to make clear	light up or illustrate
Immaculate	perfectly clean	spotless, pristine
Impasse	a deadlock, a point at which one can go no	standstill
Impediment	an obstacle, something in the way	obstruction
Imperial	like royalty	royal, regal
Imperious	arrogant, behaving like royalty	commanding, overbearing
Impervious	1) unable to pass or enter, 2) unable to upset	impermeable, impenetrable
Implicate	to involve in; to connect with or be related to	involvement, connection
Implore	to beg or ask earnestly	ask, beg
Imply	to express indirectly	suggest
Inarticulate	unable to speak or express clearly	tongue-tied, unclear
Inclination	preference or tendency	tendency
Incompetent	not able to do something properly	inept, unskilled
Incumbent	1) someone who is currently holding a political position; 2) necessary	1) office-holder 2) necessary
Indictment	a charge or accusation of a serious crime	charge, accusation
Indifferent	having no particular interest in something	unconcerned
Indignant	feeling angry or insulted from an injustice	resentful, disgruntled, discontented
Inevitable	certain to happen	unavoidable
Infamous	being famous for a bad reason; having a bad reputation	notorious, scandalous
Ingenuous	innocent, sincere, naïve	innocent, trusting
Ingenuity	innovation, creativity	inventiveness, creativity
Innate	born with, not learned	natural
Innovative	introducing something new, creative	ingenious, novel, original, creative
Inquiry	a question or request for information	question, investigation
Inscribe	to write or etch words on or into a surface	write, carve, etch, engrave
Insinuation	a sneaky suggestion of something bad	suggestion, hint
Insipid	boring or tasteless	uninteresting, dull, flavorless
Insolent	rude, disrespectful	impertinent, impudent
Intangible	not able to be touched or sensed; impossible to understand, unknown	untouchable, not physical
Integrate	to bring together	combine, merge
Integrity	a person's moral character	honesty, honor
Intrepid	fearless and adventurous	fearless, brave, courageous
Intricate	complex	complicated, very detailed
Invigorate	to fill with strength and energy	energize, revive, revitalize
Irate	very very angry	furious
Ironic	saying one thing, but meaning the opposite, sometimes as a form of humor	sarcastic
Irrefutable	impossible to deny	undeniable
Irreverent	disrespectful	scornful, disdainful
Itinerant	nomadic, constantly moving	transient, nomadic
Jargon	the specialized language or vocabulary	lingo, language
Jeer	to make fun of or insult someone	mock, taunt, ridicule
Jest	to joke	joke
Jubilant	overly joyful	exultant joyful
Juxtapose	contrasting two very different things	compare, contrast
Keen	sharp-witted and intelligent	sharp, observant, perceptive
Kinetic	moving	dynamic, energized
Laden	weighed down with a large amount of something, burdensome	loaded, burdened
Lament	to express grief, to mourn	groan, weep, mourn
Languid	slow-moving	relaxed slow, unenergetic
Laud	to praise	extol, exalt
Laudatory	expressing praise	praising, extolling
lavish	extravagant; spending a lot or giving a lot	luxurious, grand, expensive
Lax	careless	lazy

Leach	to wash or dissolve away	drain
Leer	a look or gaze in an unpleasant or malicious way	ogle
Lenient	tolerant, merciful, generous,	forgiving, relaxed
Linger	to delay or be slow in leaving	remain, continue, stay
Livid	discolored, bruised, or very angry	enraged, furious
Locomotion	motion	movement
Loquacious	talkative	garrulous, talkative
Lush	full of plant life	abundant
Maladroit	clumsy	awkward, incompetent
Malevolence	meanness or hatred	meanness, hatred, badness
Mar	to ruin	spoil
Mercurial	characterized by rapid and unpredictable change	volatile, capricious, temperamental
Merge	to blend together	combine, blend, integrate
Meticulous	careful, paying attention to details	conscientious, immaculate
Mirth	happiness and good cheer	cheerfulness, merriment
Misconstrue	misinterpret	misunderstand
Miserly	cheap	frugal, thrifty
Mitigate	to make less severe; to moderate; to lessen the effect of something	alleviate, reduce, diminish
Molten	melted	liquid
Monotonous	boring	tedious, dull, unexciting
Nautical	related to sailing or the sea	naval, maritime, seagoing
Nimble	agile and flexible	lithe, quick
Nonchalant	without concern	calm, cool, unconcerned
Notorious	known widely and unfavorably	infamous
Novice	a beginner	amateur
Noxious	harmful; poisonous	toxic
Null	zero value or nothing	void, invalid
Nullify	to make of something "zero" or to cancel the effect of something	void, invalidate
Obdurate	stubborn	adamant, obstinate
Objective	not influenced by personal opinion	unbiased, nonpartisan
Obscure	hidden; hard to see or understand	unclear, hidden
Obsolete	out of date, no longer useful	old fashioned, outdated
Obstinate	stubborn	adamant, obdurate
Obstruction	a barrier or obstacle	impediment
Ominous	threatening or foreshadowing something bad	threatening, baleful, menacing, sinister
Opaque	impossible to see through, preventing the passage of light	cloudy, nontransparent
Open-handed	generous	charitable, benevolent
Opulent	rich, characterized by wealth	wealthy, lavish
Oration	a formal speech	speech
Orator	public speaker	rhetorician, public speaker
Ostentatious	showy, pretentious	flamboyant, extravagant
Pact	a formal agreement between two countries	agreement
Palatable	1) agreeable 2) tasty	1) acceptable 2) appetizing
Pan	to criticize	attack, lambaste
Panacea	a solution that cures all problems	cure-all
Paramount	having superior power and influence	important
Parch	to make very thirsty	scorch, roast
Pardoned	to forgive	excuse
Parody	a humorous imitation	satire
Pedantic	overly academic, boring	scrupulous, precise
Penitent	feeling regret for doing something wrong	repentant, contrite
Penurious	poor	poverty-stricken
peripheral	1) on the edge, 2) unimportant	outer, edge
Permeate	spread	pervade
Pernicious	(adj.) extremely harmful; deadly, fatal	harmful, damaging
Perpetuate	to continue, to preserve	maintain, carry on
Peruse	to read or examine carefully	scrutinize, examine, investigate
Pilfer	to steal	plunder, steal, pillage
Pious	deeply religious	religious, devout, devoted
Placate	to quiet down, appease	appease, pacify, calm

Plaintive	sounding sad and mournful	mournful, sorrowful, wistful
Plausible	possible or believable	possible, believable, feasible
Plight	a bad situation	predicament, trouble, difficulty
Plumage	the feathers on a bird	feathers, mantle
Plunder	to steal	pillage, loot, raid
Polymorphous	having many shapes	multiform, multifarious
Posterity	future generations	progeny, descendants
Potable	suitable for drinking	drinkable
Potent	having great power or being effective	powerful, strong, effective
Pragmatic	practical or useful	practical, sensible, realistic
Preamble	an introduction to a formal document	introduction
Precedence	being more important than something or someone else	priority
Predominantly	being larger in number, quantity, power, status	prevailing
Premise	a summary or conclusion	assumption, hypothesis
Presume	to assume	assume
Primitive	1) having to do with an early stage of some development 2) simple	1) early, primary 2) plain, basic
Privation	lack of necessities	hardship, destitution, poverty
Procure	to obtain	achieve, get,
Profane	to treat someone/something with disrespect	debase, degrade
Profanity	offensive language	swear word, obscenity, curse
Prolific	1) productive 2) plentiful	1) creative, productive 2) abundant
Propagate	to reproduce or multiply	grow, breed, spread, increase
Prophetic	predicting the future	prescient
Prosperous	wealthy or fortunate	thriving, successful
Provisional	existing in the present, possibly to change in the future	temporary, conditional
Prudent	careful and well-planned	wise, careful, shrewd
Pugnacious	quick to fight or argue	hostile, aggressive, combative, antagonistic
Pungent	a strong, sharp taste or smell	strong, aromatic
Purist	a person who insists on following traditions and rules	perfectionist, traditionalist
Quandary	problem	dilemma, predicament
Quarrelsome	argumentative	bickering, confrontational
Quell	1) to calm 2) to stop	1) subdue, pacify, 2) end, crush
Quibble	to complain about little things	grumble, complain
Quiver	to tremble	shake, shiver, quaver
Ramble	to move or speak without direction	chatter, babble, meander
Rancid	having a nasty smell or taste, rotting	sour, rotten, stale, putrid
Rancorous	showing hatred or ill-will	bitter, spiteful, hateful, resentful
Ratify	to approve, usually a law	confirm, endorse, approve
Ravenous	extremely hungry	starving, famished
Rebuke	to criticize sharply	admonish, scold, castigate
Recalcitrant	disobedient	uncooperative, intractable
Recede	to move away or become smaller	retreat, diminish, decrease
Recluse	someone who lives a solitary life and tends to avoid others	hermit
Recreation	something done for fun like a hobby or game	leisure, fun
Recuperate	to heal or return to good health	recover
rehabilitate	to restore to good condition (usually through therapy or education)	restore, renew, fix
Relic	ancient object	artifact
Relinquish	to renounce	give up
Reminisce	to think of the past	recollect, remember
Remote	distant	far away, secluded
Renaissance	a rebirth or revival	resurgence
Rendezvous	a meeting, usually in secret	meeting, appointment, tryst
Renege	to go back on a promise or contract	retract, go back on
Renounce	to give up or resign something	reject, relinquish
Repent	to feel sorry and regretful	regret, rue
Replete	filled with something	abundant, full
Repugnant	highly disgusting	offensive
Residual	left over, remaining	remaining, excess, persisting
Retrospect	review of past events	hindsight

Revere	to deeply respect or admire	respect, esteem, appreciation
Reverent	respectful, worshipful	respectful, worshipping, admiring
Rhetorician	public speaker	orator
Rift	1) a narrow crack in something 2) a break in friendly relations	1) split, crack 2) quarrel, fight
Rigor	1) the quality of being challenging 2) the quality of being inflexible	1) challenge 2) strictness, severity
Rigorous	1) challenging 2) inflexible	1) difficult 2) strict, severe
Robust	strong and healthy	powerful, vigorous
Rout	defeat	retreat, conquer, vanquish
Rue	to regret	regret, lament
Ruse	a clever trick	ploy, scheme
Salutation	greeting	welcome, hail, greeting
Salve	something used to heal or soothe	ointment, treatment, cure
Sanctimonious	acting morally superior, holier-than-thou	pious, self-righteous
Sarcastic	using witty language used to insult or show displeasure	sardonic, ironic, satirical
Satire	the use of humor, irony, or exaggeration	sarcasm, mockery, parody
Scold	to criticize	reprimand, admonish, rebuke
Scorn	lack of respect accompanied by a feeling of dislike	contempt, dislike
Scornful	A strong feeling of dislike	contemptuous
Scourge	someone or something that causes others trouble or suffering	affliction, problem, curse
scruples	feelings of doubt or guilt about a suggested action	hesitation, reservation, reluctance, second thoughts
Scrutinize	to examine closely	peruse, inspect, study
Sedate	to calm, especially by use of drug	tranquilize, calm
Shrewd	very clever and smart, tricky	astute, sharp-witted, intelligent
Slander	a false and mean-spirited statement meant to harm someone's reputation	defamation, lie, untruth, insult
Solemn	not cheerful or smiling; very serious	serious, sober, somber, dignified
Solidify	strengthen	reinforce, bolster
Somber	serious, dark, or gloomy	dark, dull, gloomy, solemn
Sporadic	having no pattern or order	irregular, random, infrequent
Sprawl	to sit, lie, or fall with one's arms and legs spread out	lounge, lie
Spur	to encourage or incentivize someone or some action	stimulate, encourage, support
Spurious	fake or false	invalid, illegitimate, fictitious
Squalid	extremely dirty and unpleasant	filthy, grimy, improper
Squander	to waste something	waste, throw away, misuse
Stagnate	to become inactive or dull	stand, do nothing, not move
Staid	straitlaced and serious	quiet, steady, rule-following, boring
Stark	bare, without decoration	somber, gloomy, undecorated, uninviting
Steadfast	loyal and constant	committed, faithful, devoted, unwavering, unswerving
Stifle	to hold back or smother	suffocating, smothering, suppressing, restraining
Subjective	influenced by personal opinion	biased, partisan
Sublime	very beautiful or perfect	awesome, wonderful
Succinct	briefly and clearly expressed	concise, short, brief
Superficial	1) on or near the surface 2) fake	1) shallow 2) false, inauthentic
Superfluous	more than what is required or needed	unnecessary, extra, redundant
Surmise	to believe that something is true without having evidence to confirm it	guess, conjecture, suspect
Surrogate	a substitute	replacement, proxy
Sustain	to support	assist, help, encourage
Taxing	requiring a lot of effort (either physically or mentally)	exhausting, demanding
Temperament	your usual mood or behavior	personality, disposition
Tenacious	holding on to something strongly and persistently	persistent, determined
Tepid	neither hot nor cold	lukewarm, unenthusiastic
Thesis	a statement that summarizes the claim of an argument	theory, claim, argument
Thorough	done with great care and completeness	meticulous, scrupulous
Thrifty	able to handle money wisely, not extravagant	prudent, economical, frugal
Timid	showing a lack of courage or confidence	reserved, shy, meek, bashful
Toil	to work hard	labor
Tome	a book, especially a long and scholarly one	opus, book, publication, novel

Transgress	to go beyond a limit or boundary; to disobey	misbehave, act out, disobey
Transgression	a violation of a law, command, or duty	offense, crime, wrongdoing
Transient	temporary	impermanent, fleeting
Translucent	almost transparent, able to be seen through clearly	colorless, clear see-through, transparent
Transpose	transfer something to a different place or context	exchange, switch, relocate, interchange
Trivial	unimportant	unimportant, insignificant, minor
Trumpet	to announce or declare something for all to hear	proclaim, broadcast
Tryst	a secret meeting	rendezvous
Unscrupulous	having or showing no moral principles; not honest or fair; dishonest	corrupt, immoral, dishonest
Vacuous	empty	blank, vacant, dumb
Variegated	having many parts or colors	multicolored, varicolored
Vend	to sell	sell
Venerate	to regard with deep respect	revere, respect
Veneration	great respect	reverence, respect, admiration
Verbatim	using exactly the same words	word for word
Versatile	able to do many things well	adaptable, flexible
Vexation	discomfort or distress	annoyance, irritation, irritability
Vicarious	experienced in the imagination through feelings and actions of another person	indirect, secondhand
Vigor	strength, and energy	robustness, stamina
Virtuoso	a person with great skill, especially a musician	maestro, genius, expert
Vital	necessary or essential	essential, indispensable, crucial
Vivid	very distinct or realistic	realistic, evocative, bright, colorful
Volatile	explosive and unstable	explosive, turbulent
Voracious	having a huge appetite, greedy, ravenous; excessively eager	insatiable, unquenchable, unappeasable
Waft	to float easily and gently in the air; drift	floating, drifting, gliding
Wane	1) to decrease gradually; 2) weakening in power/size/importance	disappear, decrease, diminish, dwindle, shrink
Whimsical	determined by chance or fancy instead of reason	fanciful, playful, impulsive, capricious
Wily	cunning and crafty	shrewd, clever, astute, sharp, smart
Writhe	to twist	squirm, wriggle
Zenith	the highest point	apex, acme

Write Your Own:

You may come across new words in your school, your reading, or other practice tests. Write them down here. If you write down new words, you'll have an extra-complete list to study from. The more words you know, the more prepared you'll be for the test.

Word	Definition	Synonyms

Answer Key

The First Section

1. Admonished
2. Acclimate
3. Academic
4. Adhere
5. Abdicated
6. Abhor
7. Adept
8. Aggregate
9. Adjunct
10. Admire

1. Detestable
2. Abhorrent
3. Shorten
4. Forgive
5. Restraint
6. Plentiful
7. Pit
8. Accumulate
9. Agreement
10. Proverb
11. Obdurate
12. Glue
13. Challenge
14. Worsen
15. Annoy

The Second Section

1. Appalled
2. Arduous
3. Amiable
4. Arid
5. Archaic
6. Animosity
7. Amass
8. Altruistic
9. Aristocrat
10. Antagonize

1. Hurt
2. Related
3. Assert
4. Shy
5. Vague
6. Uncertain
7. Improve
8. Shapeless
9. Critical
10. Pain
11. Escapade
12. Indifference
13. Capability
14. Eloquent
15. Deceit

The Third Section

1. Berated
2. Ascended
3. Authentic
4. Assessed
5. Barbed
6. Bashful
7. Assailable
8. Asserted
9. Baleful
10. Bedeviled

1. Goal
2. Diligent
3. Shrewd
4. Achievement
5. Loud
6. Enlarge
7. Commanding
8. Boring
9. Flood
10. Resent
11. Falsify
12. Aggressive
13. Helpful
14. Goodness
15. Harmless

The Fourth Section

1. Cautious
2. Brig
3. Biased
4. Circulated
5. Cacophony
6. Cast Away
7. Brackish
8. Blight
9. Bewildered
10. Bolster

1. Bold
2. Brackish
3. Bully
4. Growing
5. Strong
6. Disastrous
7. Truthful
8. Honesty
9. Unpredictable
10. Scold
11. Disappointment
12. Abyss
13. Annoyed
14. Record
15. Wary

The Fifth Section

1. Clarity
2. Contempt
3. Cognizant
4. Console
5. Comprehensive
6. Consensus
7. Congenial
8. Coalesced
9. Clandestine
10. Construe

1. Force
2. Think
3. Initialization
4. Shared
5. Capable
6. Laziness
7. Control
8. Surrender
9. Patronize
10. Accept
11. Imprisonment
12. Obey
13. Bewilder
14. Thicken
15. Diligent

The Sixth Section

1. Crevice
2. Cordially
3. Decomposes
4. Deleterious
5. Counsel
6. Correlation
7. Delusional
8. Cumulative
9. Defer
10. Contradicted

1. Disdainful
2. Debatable
3. Bordering
4. Regretful
5. Remorse
6. Normal
7. Overweight
8. Delay
9. Weakening
10. Expose
11. Order
12. Infer
13. Lacking
14. Adept
15. Shy

The Seventh Section

1. Despair
2. Derelict
3. Elaborate
4. Dormant
5. Dreaded
6. Deplorable
7. Dubious
8. Discern
9. Dispute
10. Deteriorating

1. Delay
2. Confinement
3. Critic
4. Agility
5. Honor
6. Weaken
7. Dirty
8. Invalidate
9. Fake
10. Criticize
11. Temperament
12. Twist
13. Energetic
14. Narcissist
15. Exit

The Eighth Section

1. Emanated
2. Elicit
3. Euphony
4. Entrepreneur
5. Evacuate
6. Eradicate
7. Era
8. Embroidered
9. Equates
10. Empathetic

1. Extend
2. Ban
3. Rudimentary
4. Imitate
5. Mystery
6. Arise
7. Embody
8. Era
9. Identical
10. Fade
11. Scholarly
12. Bliss
13. Fleeting
14. Elicit
15. Worsen

The Ninth Section

1. Fluctuate
2. Excavate
3. Frank
4. Extinct
5. Exuberant
6. Frugal
7. Fathom
8. Exquisite
9. Fundamental
10. Feasible

1. Annoy
2. Ban
3. Banish
4. Praise
5. Embroider
6. Aspect
7. Falsehood
8. Bliss
9. Wild
10. Divide
11. Ostentatious
12. Incite
13. Sink
14. Periphery
15. Merge

The Tenth Section

1. Hue
2. Gingerly
3. Illuminated
4. Imperial
5. Garrulous
6. Hasty
7. Glutton
8. Impasse
9. Groveling
10. Grimace

1. Thin
2. Type
3. Splendor
4. Sociable
5. Hoary
6. Merriment
7. Old
8. Shack
9. Peculiarity
10. Contemptible
11. Spotless
12. Obstruction
13. Commanding
14. Impermeable
15. Involve

The Eleventh Section

1. Integrity
2. Intangible
3. Incompetent
4. Infamous
5. Innovative
6. Intricate
7. Indifferent
8. Intrepid
9. Insolent
10. Inevitable

1. Beg
2. Suggest
3. Ill-expressed
4. Tendency
5. Office-holder
6. Accusation
7. Discontent
8. Trusting
9. Innovative
10. Natural
11. Investigation
12. Engrave
13. Implication
14. Boring
15. Merge

The Twelfth Section

1. Jargon
2. Irate
3. Jests
4. Linger
5. Lax
6. Jubilant
7. Invigorated
8. Lamented
9. Lauded
10. Lavish

1. Sarcastic
2. Undeniable
3. Scornful
4. Transient
5. Taunt
6. Contrast
7. Observant
8. Dynamic
9. Burdened
10. Relaxed
11. Celebrated
12. Relaxed
13. Drain
14. Ogle
15. Irate

The Thirteenth Section

1. Nautical
2. Novice
3. Marred
4. Meticulous
5. Loquacious
6. Malevolence
7. Mirth
8. Noxious
9. Obdurate
10. Nullify

1. Movement
2. Abundant
3. Clumsy
4. Volatile
5. Coalesce
6. Misinterpret
7. Cheap
8. Alleviate
9. Melted
10. Tedious
11. Lithe
12. Calm
13. Infamous
14. Void
15. Unbiased

The Fourteenth Section

1. Obstructing
2. Pardoned
3. Opulent
4. Peripheral
5. Pact
6. Ominous
7. Panacea
8. Pernicious
9. Palatable
10. Orator

1. Unknown
2. Outdated
3. Adamant
4. Nontransparent
5. Generous
6. Speech
7. Flamboyant
8. Criticize
9. Important
10. Roast
11. Imitation
12. Boring
13. Contrite
14. Poor
15. Spread

The Fifteenth Section

1. Peruse
2. Plumage
3. Premise
4. Presumed
5. Preamble
6. Plausible
7. Pilfering
8. Potable
9. Placate
10. Plight

1. Maintain
2. Religious
3. Mournful
4. Pillage
5. Amorphous
6. Progeny
7. Powerful
8. Practical
9. Priority
10. Prevailing
11. Basic
12. Hardship
13. Achieve
14. Debase
15. Obscenity

The Sixteenth Section

1. Recreation
2. Ravenous
3. Prudent
4. Quandary
5. Recuperate
6. Rancorous
7. Prolific
8. Pungent
9. Prosperous
10. Recluse

1. Multiply
2. Prescient
3. Conditional
4. Hostile
5. Traditionalist
6. Argumentative
7. Pacify
8. Complain
9. Tremble
10. Chatter
11. Rotting
12. Approve
13. Scold
14. Disobedient
15. Diminish

The Seventeenth Section

1. Reminisce
2. Rue
3. Salutation
4. Replete
5. Retrospect
6. Remote
7. Revere
8. Rigorous
9. Rendezvous
10. Relic

1. Restore
2. Renounce
3. Revival
4. Retract
5. Relinquish
6. Apologize
7. Disgusting
8. Remaining
9. Worshipful
10. Orator
11. Crack
12. Challenge
13. Strong
14. Vanquish
15. Ploy

The Eighteenth Section

1. Scolded
2. Solemn
3. Squander
4. Sporadically
5. Sedate
6. Scrutinized
7. Stark
8. Spurred
9. Sprawled
10. Stagnate

1. Ointment
2. Self-righteousness
3. Ironic
4. Sarcasm
5. Contempt
6. Contemptuous
7. Affliction
8. Reservations
9. Astute
10. Lie
11. Strengthen
12. Gloomy
13. Fictitious
14. Dirty
15. Serious

The Nineteenth Section

1. Sublime
2. Surmised
3. Tepid
4. Timid
5. Succinctly
6. Temperament
7. Thoroughly
8. Transient
9. Stifle
10. Transgressions

1. Loyal
2. Biased
3. Fake
4. Unnecessary
5. Substitute
6. Support
7. Toilsome
8. Determined
9. Claim
10. Economical
11. Labor
12. Book
13. Disobey
14. Clear
15. Transfer

The Twentieth Section

1. Zenith
2. Wane
3. Trivial
4. Virtuoso
5. Whimsical
6. Wafted
7. Versatile
8. Vexation
9. Trumpeted
10. Vend

1. Rendezvous
2. Corrupt
3. Empty
4. Multicolored
5. Revere
6. Respect
7. Identical
8. Annoy
9. Robust
10. Essential
11. Colorful
12. Explosive
13. Insatiable
14. Cunning
15. Twist

Made in United States
Troutdale, OR
10/05/2024